EYES OF

I

IF ALL YOU SEE IS THE BEAST, THEN YOU HAVEN'T SEEN

YOURSELF…

STEVE ELLÉ

For it is I

Author: Steve Ellé

Editor: M.P.R Jasmyne Daniels

Cover Design: Muhammad Javaid

Book Design: Mamoon Ajmal

Written 2019-2020

SPIRITUAL COMMANDMENT

Behold. I command that any spirit that is not of love, not of peace, not of happiness, that is not of humbleness, that is not pure and that is not free to let go of me this day. Let go of my body, my mind, my spirit, and my soul.

I command for thee to flee, for I hold the power of all things that is in me. If you choose not to do so, I command for all of thee to be placed upon thee this day. For this is my commandment, for this is my will, for this is my power.

Acknowledgements

I would like to thank the creator of all things for leading and guiding me through the spiritual journey as well as the physical journey while creating something that is so beautiful.

I HAVE ALL THAT I AM, FOR IT IS I...

EYES OF

I

Table of Contents

I have everything in existence and nonexistence. I have created, and so it was. I have imagined, and so it is. Who I am is not a mistake. It is I, the beholder of all things. It is I, the beholder of the universe. It is I that lives in you, for it is I that you see and do not see. For I am all power. For I am all-powerful. For I am I.

THE BEGINNING OF THE END OF THE BEGINNING...

CHAPTER 1
THEE ILLUSION (I)

There are many illusions in life. Some things that one may understand and the illusions of the things that one may not understand, but it is I. I cometh in many forms, but it is I. The understanding of oneself is the beginning of one's journey. I think it is just he or she divided, but it is I. I is everything and everything that is and will be. Before one can understand the spiritual world, one must understand thee illusion…The illusion that I see from day to day is only but an illusion. All things are working together and against one another, but it is I. The different kind of people from Africa, Korea, India, China, Mexico, and Europe are all the same as I in many forms. The world that I live in is working against I, so I may know its power. I am a test as well as an understanding. How would I know darkness if light was never revealed? But know, everything that is shown should be questioned for I may know the truth. Light reveals darkness and darkness reveals light. In this life, all things are hidden and only revealed in the spirit and not of the flesh. Therefore, it is important to let the spirit reveal its nature rather than the flesh. I put all my trust in I, the supreme and creator of all things. In this life, I am here to understand so I may know and listen to that inner voice of the creator of all things that is in me. The world that I live in is a test so I may know thy self. If I am listening to the inner peace. Everything in the flesh will be revealed. But if I am living in the flesh, then I am asleep and living in the illusion. Know thy sheep by thy spirit but not by thy flesh (the illusion). The body is only a makeup of I, but "I" is I. There are many worlds—the world of the illusion and the world of the spirit that is infinite. Which world am I living in? What world do I see and hear? What is in the spirit, and what is in the flesh? There is spiritual food and fleshly food. This is one of the reasons why fleshly food does not hold as thee illusion. In the world of the illusion, everything is divided. The majority of people are working for money, which is an illusion. Money does not exist; it is only but an illusion. If I give money power, then I am asleep and living happily in the illusion. The illusion is only a fairy tale; it is make-believe, which is a lie. I am being tested; I have always been tested. For every great test, there is growth in knowing. If I ever find myself repeating the same pattern, then the test is being repeated due to my lack of understanding. Once a test has been passed, another test is given for growth in the spirit. When I have realized that I have been tested, then I have truly begun my journey.There are many illusions in life, some that I know and some that are hidden. The illusion of religion is to believe in something. But know, there is a difference in believing and knowing. When I believe something, the information of knowing stops, and I have no intention of knowing the truth due to my belief. But, when I know something, the Creator has revealed it to me in many forms. The deeper I am in the spirit, the deeper of knowing is revealed. I should always know thy self. Religion is a part of the illusion; it has divided the people and put I against one another. It has forced me to believe but not to know the truth. Religion is another trick that is deceiving. All things of peace come with love, and all things of love come with peace. There are many tests in life that come in many forms of the things I desire. Lust after the spirit and not after the flesh. For the things of the flesh are a part of the illusion. Humble so you came, humble so you will be, and humble so shall you go. The world of the illusion is only for a season. The spiritual world is eternal. The illusion was made for the dead, who are asleep to the system. It is time for me to wake up and see what is in the spirit. The Creator is talking, but are you listening? Listen to that spiritual voice of the Creator that is coming in many forms of your life. It is time for me to go in the spiritual world. It is time. Know thy sheep by thy spirit but not thy flesh. The illusion loves to give people titles, anything to divide I against one another. This is another trick of the illusion. Things like boss, senator, President, and so on. The things to divide I against one another and bring confusion. The spirit of separation is a part of the wicked. The spirit of Black against White is a part of the wicked. The spirit of racism is evil and is a part of the dead. The spirit of religion is evil and is a part of the dead. This book has cometh to

3

you as a great warning. If thy bow down to these evil spirits, then so will you partake of evil. It is time that I awaken and live in the spirit and come out the flesh. For the flesh is only for a season. For what I see as my reality will soon become a dream, and my dreams will soon become reality. I cometh in many forms so he may know. Listen first and then speak for your own understanding to know the truth. It is I, for everything that will be and everything that is, for it is I. The spirit of the illusion comes in many forms of hiding itself from showing you the truth. The impure spirit has a need to pretend, which is the pretender. If you are asleep, you have chosen not to be awakened, and if you are awakened, you have heard my voice in many forms. The ideal of darkness and light is but an illusion. The world ideal of love is an illusion. No man has seen the spirit of love fulfilled. Real love has nothing to do with the illusion, and real peace has nothing to do with the illusion. My love is much greater than what the eye can see or what I can see in the spirit. The illusion cometh in the form of the giver and the taker. Listen o' this day, my children, before it is too late. Peace without love is dead, and love without peace is dead. I am all things that the eye can see and what the eye cannot see. I am all that I AM. It is I. I am the great deep, the deepest on many and all levels of life. I am the greatest of all the oceans of waters and living waters. All that you do in the illusion, may it come with peace and give love as I. The impure spirit of religion has forced me to believe but not to know the truth. The process of knowing is the process of

4

understanding. But, when I believe, the ideal of knowing stops due to my belief in the system. But know, the process of the illusion is especially important. In the beginning, everyone is asleep, as a baby in the womb of his mother, but one day, that baby will awaken, as he does in the spirit. Every man should awaken at least twice in his life. You see that baby keeps falling back asleep and continues to awaken as you shall in the spirit. The stages of awakening continue, for the growth as from a boy to a man, until he is old and will soon depart from the body back to the spirit of the Creator.

~TIME~Time in the spirit does not exist. In the illusion, it has purpose. Everything revolves around time, everything in the illusion. Even though this is the illusion, everything has purpose, even in the illusion. Everything has a time period in this life, but know, in the spirit, everything is timeless. The time within itself is a test in the fleshly body. If a man does not respect time, then he doesn't respect life or himself because life is the Creator. So, the religion has taught the people to skip the time of knowing the truth but not to know the truth. Believing is to hope for, but when you know, it is the process of understanding the ideal to know or to be awakened. The awakening is in the understanding of the illusion, which is the process to know, and that process is time. Most spirits that are asleep value money, but it is time you should value. Every time the clock ticks, it is time on the body.

Money is used to grow your flesh, but time is used to grow your spirit. The time of understanding, of knowing. The biggest illusion is money, but it is time you should value. Do not take your time away for money; it is only but an illusion. I must see through the illusion so that I understand, so that I may know. Remember, everything in the illusion is hidden, so you must begin to look through the illusion with your spirit. Seek within, for it is I that is with you and have always been with you from the womb of your mother. For I see all and in all, hidden and not hidden. Go within and seek within, and I will hear you this day. Children of the land of the illusion, it is time to come home to realization. For I am here in the darkness, in the light, in your darkest days. I am here to bring peace, for I am sorrow, for I am the hot and the cold. It is I for your own understanding. Men have divided all colors for I am all colors, as one. The impure spirit of the illusion has separated all colors to show one great color, but I am all colors. What great power will one have with only one color? I am more than what meets the eye and does not meet the eye. It is my Great Power that is all around you. It is I. I have put forth the time to allow for your own understanding so you may know. Flesh put money on you, but I put time on you. Time is the biggest test any man will face. But understand, money is the by-product for your time. If I give my time away, I have chosen not to know thy self. A rich man of the flesh is focused on the money, but the Creator of All Things is focused on your time because the money is only an illusion and is foolishness. So, ask yourself, what have I done with my time? What have I learned about I? What have you learned? A man is forgotten for his time, not for I, but for he has forgotten himself. For it is I. No amount of money can bring him peace, so he is alone, so he is forgotten. A poor man knows more about I because he had a lot of time to spend with himself. The money is a trap for the people who are asleep. A man who cannot control his ego or his emotions becomes his own downfall. A lot of you are lost souls and still are asleep in the forbidden wilderness. It is time for you to come home, my dearly beloved children. Come home to a beautiful world that I have prepared for you in the spirit. Listen this day, while you still have time.

THE VOID...

The world we are living in looks for love to fulfill the void but does not realize that we are that void; we have created that void. For that void is the curse that is in us.

Know thy self and love thy self. Why should you love thy self? You are not looking for someone else to love you. Know, when you are looking for someone else to love you, you have given your love away to someone else to control your emotions and feelings. You can never be happy because you look for someone else to bring you happiness, and this is not true love. True happiness and true love come from within. If anyone looks for you to love them, it is because they do not love self. So, if you do not love self, it means that there is an emptiness of hate for self, which is hidden. This is another trick of the illusion. If everyone loves thy self, there would be no violence. Violence only happens when you do not have love for self. For someone else to love you and for one to except means you are being held by that other being. But if we have love for self, it means that we show our love and express our love without a return or fulfillment in the external world. So, I must stop giving away MY love but express my love. I express my love by doing something nice for someone. But I give my love away when I expect for you to love me. Listen this day while you still have time! To expect love from someone other than self is a form of control! That other spirit has the power to control your emotions and your feelings at any given time. It can make you feel good or it can make you feel bad. This is why it is very important to know thy self. Know that other spirit that sits amongst you. Know who you are. Know the power that is in YOU.

The world of the illusion gives you a man or a woman to love until death do you part. But know, if he does not love self, he can never love you. If she never loves self, she can never love you. As I stated before, you should only express your love for self from within. True love does not exist in the illusion but is to be his or her expression as a light that shines upon thee. So, you ask, where is this true love? Where is this peace? The true love is within. I am that love, and I am that peace. It is in my power. I have the power to create this love. We must tell ourselves, "I AM LOVE," "I AM PEACE." There is nothing in this world that can give me something that I already have. I have the power to create whatsoever I choose. If I have not, I have chosen not. I say that to say this: no one can love you but YOU. It is in your power; it is up to you. If you choose not, then you have chosen to live in the void. Remember, in the beginning, everything was in the void without form, but there is still life, even in the void. That void is in you, at a lower realm, which is a lower state of being. That world that you have chosen, that world you have created. It is in you but is being relived over and over in different worlds and in different bodies. We must awaken from the void within us. Come out of the curse and come on up to a higher realm in the spirit if you choose. I love myself enough to do so and to be love. It is time to bring your spirit up to a higher state of being.

In order to find the truth in something, compare it with life itself, and then bring it from within you to reveal the truth. All things that you can ever imagine are within you. There is nothing in this world that you do not already have, nothing. You have the power to create everything you want; it is given to you as a free will. Whatsoever he chooses, so it is, and so is he. The power of one is much greater than what one can ever imagine.

To be asleep in the illusion is to be asleep in the spirit, and to be awakened in this illusion is to be awakened in the spirit. All that I am now, I am living as this in my own spirit. All that I know in this illusion and love in this illusion, I am without in the spirit. I am lost in my own spirit; I am without knowledge of knowing thy self. All that I love in this illusion, I have created this within my own spirit. I have cursed my own spirit. I have forgotten myself. I have created this new world. I have created this illusion. I have created my next journey. I have created my next life. I have created my next experience. A journey of oneself is the creation of oneself. All that I see, I have created these things to be, whether in this life or in a past life, but it is I. The things I see are the things I create, and the things I do not see are the things I have chosen not to create, but it is I, the things that I see. The things that I love, I once was, and things that I hate, I once was in many lives, but the things that I love are the things I have created and are the things that cause me to hate. The illusion comes in the form of love but is nothing but an illusion of loving the things of the flesh. To love the things that are unclean to the spirit. It is important to keep your spirit clean at all times. The illusion is creating things by the day for you to love, but these things are toxic to your spirit. Know thy self, and you will know the things that are in your spirit and the things to come. True love is a spirit, and evil is a spirit. The more you free yourself from the illusion, the more you will enter the things of the spirit. We must watch the things that we love because the things that we love can become evil spirits, which are unseen to the physical eye.

The physical part of love is made to hold the other person in the physical form, which is a spirit. The spiritual part of love for self in spirit is freedom, which is free will.

When I express my love, I can see when you are in the spirit of love. Real love comes from within and should only be the expression in the illusion. But when one is in the spirit of love, he is surrounded by love. To be in love with something in the illusion becomes an idol for you to worship. An idol for you to follow, to abide and to lead. It becomes a model of your everyday life, but true love from within is freedom. The love of the illusion is bondage, and you are made as a slave to be controlled by the system. It is time to lift your spirit and free your spirit. You are only free if you choose.

The system ideal to be perfect is to be like me. To act the way I act, to do the evil things I do. If you do not do these things, you are considering to be imperfect for me. So, one may say, "I don't understand you. I don't know you." What is the word perfect? It is a word made by the system to make a person go crazy. Made to never except a person but to always look down upon other people because we do not understand them. Another form of being perfect is the system's ways in its holidays, race, birthdays, and its laws, to be a part of a system that programs you to act a certain way. But if you go outside of this system, then you are imperfect. The word perfect is made to cause confusion because to truly to be perfect is to be free, and to be free is to be a part of I.

To truly see the illusion is to truly see yourself, and to see yourself is to see the power of I.

CHAPTER 2
THE MIND OF A SLAVE

The system has made you what you are and what you will be. This is the mind of a slave. Back then, it was physical slavery; today it is slavery of the mind. If a man does not control his mind, then someone else will.

A slave is made by numbers, which is order and control. One's mind with numbers, such as time, money, age, events, and so on. This is a form of control in the system. How is a man powerful if he does not have control over his own mind?

We are taught to be a slave from birth. From the time you enter into your mother's womb, you have entered into the system. In this illusion, you have been taught to be a slave to everything you know and everything you have ever known in this body since you were a baby. It is the mentality of the mind of a slave. So, you ask, how is this possible? How is everything that you have been taught the mind of a slave? Let us first begin with your race. Where did you come from? Where are you from? This is putting you in a box. This is dividing you. This is putting you amongst certain people. This is the same as when the slaves were put in a certain group with other slaves that were common. It is the same as putting like-minded people, like racists, in the society together. They feel more comfortable because they are of the same race or mindset. This is my brother, or this is my sister. Maybe this person will understand me a little bit more because we are of the same race. But the reality is, the person that you feel is your brother can be against you. The whole time, we intend to do things we do not want to do but we do these things because we feel that this person is the same race as I, so we feel they can relate to I, but in reality, it is nothing but an illusion. This is something the system has made for you to feel comfortable with. The things you do not want to do but end up doing because you see someone of the same race as I. As you have been taught in the system, you are this race, so you feel more comfortable in doing the job even more because you see someone of the same race doing it. This is the same with as names. Names are another form of us being divided, to define you as this one particular person. I know many of us intend to have a nickname because we are tired of being in a box. These nicknames are names you might call your brother or your sister. But when you give yourself one name in this system, this is another form of slavery. To keep you as this person only and nothing else. You cannot be anything else because you only have this one particular name that was given to you by the system. The system has blinded you; it has misguided you. The system has put you in a box of this illusion. Even things like where are you from.

A person may say, "I am from Europe," and another person says, "I am from the U.S." These are other forms that are putting you in a box because you are blinded by where you are from. You feel as if this is your abiding place. You feel as if, when you live in this place, you are at home. You feel more comfortable thinking that this is really your home, that you are really from North America or Africa. These are all illusions, all a part of putting you in a box to make you a slave. This is also the case with the color of your skin. Whether your skin is light or darker, we make these things apart of us and think that this is really us. Or we say things like, "I'm Irish," or, "I'm Italian," and we feel privileged to be such but not realizing that these things were made by the system for us to fight amongst each other, for us to be divided amongst each other. This is a form of evil. This is a form of a setback. If you understand what I am saying, not looking at the actual race or what you call "tribe," then you will understand that this is made by the system and was given to you by the system. It is to put you in a mindset to be held down, to be held back, to have the mind of a slave.

The same is true with your age. A younger woman feels more comfortable around a younger woman, and an older woman feels more comfortable around an older woman. This is another way of dividing you, to put you in a box, making you think and act as a slave.

These are some of the things the system will do to play tricks on your mind. You will look at these things as if its only small but not realizing that this is what this illusion is doing to your mind. It is misguiding you. It is misleading you. It is putting you in a box, even to the point where they have even given you a social security number or national ID number. That is used to define you, to put a number on you. You may think that this is nothing major, but this number is meant to be carried and held onto. The number defines you and tells all information about you. The same as an item at the grocery store that has a skew number. That skew number is the byproduct of what you are purchasing. This is the same as your national ID or social security number. You are an item number in this system. You are a product, which means you are a slave in this system. A slave that is on the assembly line, that is working for this system as a job.

You feel as if you must work a job, so you continue going to work every day from 9am to 5pm, and you do the same routine every day. Not realizing that you are a slave, and these things are keeping you busy, so you do not have time to think or to know thy self. You do not have time to work on yourself or your spiritual growth. You are just stuck in this box of going to work every day with no sleep. You may spend more time at work than you do with your family. This is not life; this is the mind of a slave. This is a choice that is being forced upon you by the system but only if you are allowing this spirit. Therefore, we must be incredibly careful with programming from the media. They show us all these programs to show you how to act, how to walk, how to talk, how to listen, how to eat, how to dance, how to sing, and so on. They are teaching you all these things because this is all a part of putting you in a box. This is making you a slave, a slave that is made by the system as if you are a robot. You watch all these Tv programs on television from sports to basketball, football and even movies. They are programing you when you get done with work. You are rushing home to watch a football game and you do not have time to think because the system has programmed you to keep you busy.

Whether it is going to work or going to watch a basketball game, these things are designed to keep you held down. To keep you in a box from knowing thy self. From knowing who you truly are. You are not some puppet on an assembly line. You are not some robot. You have a free will to do and be whatsoever you choose. The system will keep you in a slave mindset, brainwashing your mind. Even the news is used to program you with negativity. All you see is negative because they want to keep you in a negative mindset. You are in a place where you are not positive because all you see is negative. Music and movies that speak about violence or this false love are 95% negative. The system has constantly been brainwashing you to be a slave or a puppet for the system. They are taking you back into the void. The system wants you to be this evil and negative person because this system is sucking all your energy and feeding on it as if it were a meal.

17

You must be incredibly careful even with the money they have given you. All people are doing is talking and thinking about money. There are almost no other discussions—either it is about a relationship or about money. Money is another form of bondage. Real love and real peace have nothing to do with money because whatsoever you like to do, you will give it away. If you like to sew, you will give clothes away to your sister or your brother. If you like to cook, you will give food to your brother or your sister. This is true love. This is true happiness. This system will mislead and misguide you, even in the way it feels. It will allow you to feel in such a way. It will allow you to feel happy at times, and it will allow you to feel sad at times. The system will have you feeling a certain way because the system is designed to control you, to program you to do, to say and to speak, and to act a certain way as if you have cut on a switch to do so. This system is designed to do so. This is why they have news programs, events, sports, and all these things to distract you because, when it's time for you to act a certain way, they want you to be in line.

Think about the holidays. They want you to stand in lines. They want you to be programmed to shop on certain days, to only shop on Christmas, Valentine's Day, and birthdays. The system is programming you to do certain things on certain days. It is not normal to be programmed by a system that does not have love for you, that does not love you. This system has no love for you. It is the same when you choose a career. They never tell you to be whatever

18

you choose; they tell you what career you want, as if you are only talented in one thing. This is all an illusion to keep you in a box, to keep you away from knowing thy self. The system has made you a slave since birth. It says that you are talented at one thing to keep you in box, so you are in line with the system just as the slaves back then. Certain slaves worked in the field, and certain slaves worked in the house. This was a daily routine, the same way as a man's career which he calls his talent.

The system will also have you in the mindset of doing wrongful and evil deeds, such as obeying the law. There are certain things that you do, that you must do, and if you don't do these things, they will take you to a correctional facility or give you some type of ticket to fix the issue. This is a forceful system, such as a slave being forced to act and be a certain way. The system is forcing you to be a robot; they want you to obey. It wants you to act accordingly. Everyday you get up in the morning, it has you doing the same routine: eat breakfast in the morning, lunch in the afternoon and dinner at night. This is to have you programmed by the system to act a certain way. If you do anything differently then you are out of line; you are out of place. You are not in the right state of mind because to be normal is to really be crazy, and to be crazy is to really be normal. A system that considers you to be normal is being obedient, is being a slave without knowing. It is being asleep. It is the same with your family. This system has program you to say, "This is my family," "This is who I am," "This is where I'm from," but not realizing that the family you have are spiritual beings with whom you have the chance to experience this life. This is only physical, but on a spiritual level we are connected with all things. On a physical level, we all are divided. The system has you in a box and has you divided with your love ones, friends, and family. It even has you divided with your education level or intelligence, what you know or how much you know. The system put you in a box with all that you know with certain information and limits you on information. Everybody knows the same information. This is all part of programming you. To put you in a box where you do not know anything. You only know what the system has given you, and you feel as if you are a smart person but not realizing that you are only a good listener. The system has made you become a good listener, which you consider to be smart, but a truly smart person is a person who thinks outside the box. This is true smartness and intelligence.

This system has also lied to you about your history. They have told you that you are from here. They have told you that you are from there, but the system has made up your history, which is his story. The system has made up the story for you to believe and put it in your textbook. When you go to school, they are reading this book that they have made up, and you think that these things are true but not realizing that these things were made up by the system. The same goes for man's language that you know and speak so well; it was made up by the system. This is another form of being a slave where they put you under the spell, as the word spell. This is all a part of the system to put you in a box and put you in the place of the void, in a place to be asleep, to not to know thy self.

The system does not have love for you. The system has lie to you. The system has pretended to be your friend; it has pretended to be your brother, your father and mother. The system does not have love for you. It is telling you what is right and what is wrong. It is trying to make the choice for you, and it want you to follow it. If you are not going with the system, you are going against the system. The system does not have love for you; it pretends to, but it does not. The same way as darkness and light. They tell you what light is and what darkness is, but who is to say what is right and what is wrong? What do you feel is right deep down inside? It is not what they tell you is right but what energy you feel. What vibration do you feel? This is why it is important to know thy self, know thy ways, know thy likeness. This system has taught us to be of a certain religion and has chosen the religion for you. The system has made you this religious person and put you in a box to say, "This is my religion." Or they tell you what your religion is. What religion do you choose?

Know, the religion is already set out to be. They have given you the religions so you can pick and choose the religion that is best for you. Not realizing that it is all the system; every religion is the system. If it were not so, it would not be in the system or placed in a category.

It is all the system, whether we feel our religion is the best religion and what we do not know on a higher level of understanding that it is an illusion. We must realize that it is still the system, the system is teaching you all these things. It even teaches you to go out and do drugs, to get high, to drink alcohol. It tells you when to drink and how to drink and how often to drink.

The system does not have love for I; it continues to put I in a box. It even tells you when you are sick and how you will react. It is constantly putting you in a box of living in the void. When you come out of the system, you come into knowing your true self, knowing the true person you really are, knowing the real you rather than some system. The system is as evil as a robot or computer. It put you in a mindset of wanting to know your desires so it can destroy you and bring you to a lower vibration. It also gives you this spirit of pride, to be in a box of having a title as a carpenter or mechanic. The system will put you in a place of these titles as a pastor, a bishop, or a priest. The system will give you these titles, and again, this is another form of putting you in a box and making you a slave because the system has gotten you caught up in all these titles. In the world holidays, world religions, in this false love, false peace, false hope, false faith and false belief. The system has gotten you to go backwards rather than going forward. The system does not have love for you. It pretends to be your friend, but it is not your friend. The system has given you so called "power," but you do not have power. There is no power in the system. It acts as if you have power, but you do not have power in the system. How could you have power if there are so many guidelines that you must abide by to be normal? To be normal is to lose yourself, your power, your greatness, your love, your peace, and your glory.

The system will put you in a place of not knowing, but only the things of the system. This is why we must free our minds—to free your spirit of this illusion and get back to the reason why you are here, for your spiritual growth and the true understanding of all things. This is real power, to know who you are and get out this system and out this box of being a certain way and acting a certain way. This is what the system wants us to do because he does not know himself, for he does not know I. We are not here to just work. We are not here just to be talented. To be the best I can be on a physical level, I must first become the best I can be on a spiritual level. This is why this whole reality was made, so a man can think—not so a man can do, but so a man can think. Whatsoever a man thinketh, so is he, and so it is. So, we must think about everything we do because we will become slaves within this system before we can realize it. It happens so quickly that we feel as if we are moving forward but are really moving backwards into the void, into not knowing thy self.

The spirit of pride, the spirit of success, the spirit of money, the spirit of race, the spirit of your physical appearance, the spirit of your career, the spirit of your talent, the spirit of being programmed by the system, the spirit of your family and friends, the spirit of your education, the spirit of your information, the spirit of your history, the spirit of what is right and what is wrong, the spirit of darkness and light, the spirit of your ways and understanding, the spirit of drugs, the spirit of alcohol, the spirit of sickness, the spirit of your religion, the spirit of your God, the spirit of your thoughts and personality, the spirit of your worldly desires, the spirit of having a title, and the spirit of having power of the flesh.

The spirit that is over this system pretends to be a certain race of people, but it is not. This is an impure spirit that is not even human as some of you may think. If you ever want to trap a spirit, you will have to put it in a body. Once that spirit is in a body then you will give it thee illusion to make it believe that this is real. Once the spirit gets comfortable, then you will get everything you need from that spirit.

You see, the system that you are living in has made you a slave, not only a slave but a robot that must obey law and order at all times. You are not here by mistake; this is the world that you have chosen to enter.

In order to be free, you must have self-discipline. Without self-discipline, a man could never be free because he is held down by the things that he loves or the things that he desires in the illusion, and what he desires in the illusion can also become a friend or even an enemy.

For all that you are and all that you will be, it is I. The good and the bad, for it is I. To know who you are and to know thy will, thy ways, thy self of knowing I. This is who I am and for all there is. It is I.

CHAPTER 3
THE SPIRIT

Everything I do in life is based on feeling. Feeling is very important as is one's destiny. What I visualize and what I say is creation. But how I feel is who I AM and is where I AM. I want things in life for the feeling they bring me. Everything I want is spirit. My spirit is hungry for the things of the spirit but not of the flesh. The more I know thy self, the more I can fulfill my spirit and become one as creation and the Creator. If the spirit is not being fulfilled everything I do will not be fulfilled. There is no life without the spirit of the Creator. Some of you want things in life because you think it will bring you fulfillment, but all these things are foolishness and have nothing to do with the fulfillment of the spirit. All of these things of the flesh are only a test so I may know thy spirit.

All things have happened because I have allowed it; I have created it, and for it is who I AM. If I do not want to own it, I must renew my mind and it will renew the spirit. For this is who I AM. The mind is like a filter for the spirit, for I must be careful with the things I own. All things are made in spirit first and then in the flesh, for this is who I AM. The real me is a formless spirit and has no limitations. I am a spirit that is placed in a body, for this is who I AM. My spirit is all, and it knows all things, for this is who I AM. Whatever I need is within me infinite. All things that come before me are given in the spirit first and later revealed in the flesh. The body that my spirit is in is trying to remember itself and its nature and purpose. Everything that I look for is spirit but not of the flesh, for this is who I AM. Life has taught the people to look on the outside, but life and all things have always begun within. The life that I am in is one of infinite lives. There are many forms of me in all things, in all galaxies. I am one of many, but I AM one. My fleshly eyes can only see what is in the physical world, but my spiritual eyes is infinite. My physical body is only able to feel what is in the physical world, but my spiritual body is infinite. My physical ears are only able to hear what is in the physical world, but my spiritual ears is infinite. You see, everything that is in the flesh is also given in the spirit. So, we must be careful with whom we sit with, eat with, talk to, listen to, or whom we consider to be a friend. The spiritual things are placed on this earth so you may know the truth. Sometimes you must listen to that inner feeling that is talking to you and is preparing you all at the same time. What you are feeling and have always felt. Listen so you may be more aware. The more you listen to that inner feeling, the clearer the feeling becomes. The Creator is talking to you, but are you available? The Creator has come in many forms, but are you available? Sometimes we say that this Creator has never talked to me. But know that life itself is the Creator, and life itself talks to you in many forms, but are you available?

You ask about this feeling. What is the feeling that I hunger for? What is this feeling? Know thy self, or should I say, learn thy self between the spirit of good and evil. What spirit am I in? Is it a good spirit or an evil spirit? We should know the things we seek, the true things we hunger for. The things we love or the things we hate. What kind of spirit do I bring this day? Is it a loving spirit or a spirit of hate? I should learn thy self so I may know my own spirit, so I may feel the spirit of others, or so I may feel the spirit of the great and powerful. I AM learning thy self so I may feel my own great power, so I may feel my own great glory. What I am, I must know. If I know who I am, I will know who and what is in this house, in this body. I must keep this house clean. I must keep this body clean. The more I examine this house, the more I will be able to grow in the spirit. So, ask yourself, who is in this house? What are the things that I desire? What type of people do I choose to be around? What do I consider to be peace and love? We ask ourselves or the spirit within us. That spirit that is within you, that great power that is within you. That GREAT feeling that is within you. How do I feel? What do I feel? How do I see myself?

Sometimes in life, words may fail us, or people may fail us. What do I feel is right? Not the feeling of oneself but of the All, the Creator, the Infinite, the Almighty, the Great and Powerful, the Silence, the Only. What do you feel deep within? It is time that I take control over my life, it is time that I know more about thy self. What I am, where I came from and my purpose in this life—not physical but spiritual. PAY ATTENTION and LISTEN to what you are feeling! Before anything happens, the feeling is presented and then it is revealed. You ask yourself, how is this feeling presented? It is calm but powerful and knowing of all things, and sometimes, it is not calm depending on the demand of the urgency. The urgency to be still, to not move. That feeling will come to you loud and clear if you are aware or awakened to the things of the spirit. Greatness and power are within you. It sits amongst you patiently at your will and your command. If you choose not to use the things that are in you, then you choose to be without your true self. Real power is only good if a man uses it— not for the things of the flesh but of the spirit.

The world in which you are living, people only see you for physical things. A man only sees you for how you look, how you dress, the type of vehicle you drive, and so on. But a spiritual man sees you for your spirit, the feeling that it brings. What type of energy is being bought forth in his spirit this day? What type of spirit do you feel? What type of feeling do you see? A man should always understand that spiritual energy never stays the same. It is a spirit that can change at its own free will because it is free to do whatsoever it chooses. A spirit does not belong to anything but itself.

The things that I see physically are illusions, but the things I see spiritually, it is I. I am a spirit who can do all things physically and spiritually. When you see a man jump, this is not his physical body but his spirit that is jumping. What I do physically, I do spiritually because I am free to do whatsoever I choose. The power of I is in you. The power of I is all around you. How a man feels is the spirit that he has created to be, and how a man sees things are the things that he has chosen to see. A world that I am in is a world that I have created to be. I am what I have created. It is I. So, to change your physical world, you must change your spiritual world, which is in you. To see the things that are in you is the true journey. The real journey that is within you. This is where your power begins. Explore yourself and you will see yourself. After seeing yourself, you can see others, the spirits that are around you. To feel the spirits that are amongst you. To spend time with yourself is power, to go on that journey, to explore. To discover the things that are in you and to feel that power that is in you. To find yourself, the old you. The things that I have forgotten are the things that I have buried long ago before I was here in this body. The past lives have made my spirit flow, but with the things that I have learned, I have made my spirit grow. To grow your spirit is the real purpose of life. To grow your physical is to relive the same experience over and over again as a bad dream that you have created for your own illusion—an illusion that you have chosen, an illusion that you have created.

Now, let me take you on a beautiful journey from within your spirit. I would like for you to feel your presence, to feel your spirit. Feel the power that is around you. Feel the power that is within you. Feel who you truly are. Feel your past lives. Feel the person you used to be. Feel that person you used to be when you were a baby. Can you feel that time when you were a child? When you were a little bitty baby, you did not know this system you were in, but you began to learn the ways of the system. You began to learn how to walk, how to talk, how to dress, how to do your hair, how to clean this physical body. You spent all this time learning yourself, learning this physical world. Ever since you were just a little bitty baby, you have been waiting for something new. You have continued to wait for something new but not realizing that journey that you have been waiting for is within you. That journey that you have not started in your life yet, that journey is waiting on you. That journey is waiting for you to begin.

Are you ready to begin that journey that is within you? That journey is waiting for you to come and explore what is in you. The things that are in you, the power that is on the inside of you. The journey of your past, of your past lives or what is in store for you in the future. Feel your free spirit and free will. Know that you have a free spirit. Know that you are free with abundance. There is nothing in this world that will ever please you. There is nothing in this world that will ever satisfy you because all that you need is within you. You are all that you need; it is on the inside of you. You have always been all that you need. The things that you buy in life, you are only buying the feelings of these things. You only are buying the way that it makes you feel. But the feeling has always been inside of you since the beginning. The feeling has always been inside of you, even before you were in your mother's womb. You have always had the power to create whatsoever you have chosen to create. You have always had this free will to go to different lives and to different dimensions, in different forms and in different bodies. As you have always chosen, you have always been given this free will to be free, to live the true life and not this fairy tale of this physical life. You are abundance. You are greatness. You are powerful. You are all that you need. You have always been all that you need because, any feeling that you need, all you need to do is pull that feeling out of you. Pull the feelings that you would like to feel and keep away the feelings that you do not want to feel. Only take in the feelings that you choose to have. If you choose to feel great, you should observe the way you feel at that moment and embrace that feeling. Learn that feeling and study it. How did it make you feel when you had your first car, or when you bought your first house? How did you feel? How did you feel when you graduated from college or high school? How did you feel? Did you embrace that feeling that you felt? Did you listen to your inner self? Did you see how excited you were? Did you feel the power that you had and was able to bring out of you? You were able to change your very move that quickly.

Do you notice you have control over your own emotions? You have control over your own mind. You have control over the things in your life that you see. You have control over who you allow to be in your life. My dearly beloved, you are free. You are free, and you have always been free. If you forget this very thing, then you will begin to look to the physical world for the things that are already in you. You begin to look towards the physical world for satisfaction. For the feeling that is already in you. There is nothing anyone can give you that you do not already have. You have all that you need. You have all that you want. You are every feeling that you can imagine and every feeling that you cannot imagine. You are that and some. You are even the feeling of pain, happiness, sadness, peace, loving, kindness, fulfillment, growth. You are all that you can ever imagine. Anything you want in life is not physical. All that you want has always been spirit. It has been within your spirit. When you understand this and you are able to see this, you will flow and grow into your next dimension. This is the only purpose of life. The only purpose of life is to remember who you are and to learn and to grow out of this illusion. What we are seeing is a fairy tale. This is an illusion. Nothing is real. All that you need has always been within you. Love yourself, have peace within yourself, have happiness within yourself, have gladness and excitement within yourself. You are all that you need, and all that you are, so am I. So am I. For it is I.

SPIRITUAL FEELING

The world that we are living in is selling feelings; it is selling the spirit of feelings. What do you want in this life? All that you are buying is feeling. When you buy a new car, you are not actually buying the car; you are purchasing the feeling. Whether it is an expensive car or not, you are buying the feeling that new vehicle will bring you. In luxury, it is the feeling that you are buying. If you have a husband or wife, it is the feeling that you are spending time with. If it is a new house, it is the feeling that has you in the house you are in. If it is a new job, it is the feeling that have you at that job. Everything we are buying and spending time with, we are buying and spending time with that feeling. You give into your spirit when you have excepted certain feelings that you find to be comfortable or pleasing to your spirit. Now, that feeling you are feeling, be incredibly careful because some feelings play tricks with our minds, and that evil spirit will pretend to feel good. But the whole time, you are dealing with a demon of feelings.

When eating food that tastes good, you keep eating because you like the way it tastes, and you like the feeling that it has given you, but the whole time, you are eating poison. You have become caught up in the way it tastes and the feeling that it brings. These spirits will mislead you into a trap of the spirit of feeling. This is why it is very important to understand the different kinds of feelings. Feelings are energy, and energy is spirit. Understand that what you are feeling is the true self. It is the real; it is the spiritual world. Pay close attention to what you are feeling because the illusion will lie to you about the physical things that you need in this life or say that you need these physical things, but the whole time, that energy you feel is an evil spirit. Later, we find ourselves being hypnotized by this feeling. Understand the feelings that you feel. Study the feelings that you feel because everything in this illusion that is being sold to you are feelings.

The physical catches your attention with these physical things, but it is the feeling you feel that is great and powerful. Pay attention to the feeling. Pay attention to how you feel because your spirit is telling you the type of spirit you are dealing with. Listen to your spirit. You are a free spirit, and that means you are able to feel all feelings that are presented to you, but again, study the feelings that are being presented to you. These spirits tend to play with feelings. They trick you with the illusion to sell you a feeling. It is feeling that you are being sold, and once you buy a particular item that you think you need, you will feel a void from within, a feeling that something good has left you because these evil spirits are selling you a false feeling to receive something that is real. Be incredibly careful of the feelings that you have purchased because these feelings will cause you to be without. These feelings will cause you to live within the void. Know the feelings that you feel. Feel the power of your feelings. Be incredibly careful. The spirit of feelings will sometimes come to trick you and play with your emotions. When you think it is something, the spirit will play games with your feelings and sell you a false feeling that you think is good, but the whole time it is a feeling to destroy you. KNOW YOUR SPIRIT!

With these physical eyes, you can look forward or you can look backwards, but understand and know that this is your physical vision. With your spirit, you have spiritual vision. Spiritual vision allows a person to see what is in the future and what is in the past. This is a gift that a lot you have. The future is revealed to you. The same way you hear with your physical ears, you are able to feel and hear what is in the spirit, which is the spiritual world. If you are able to listen, let your ears hear the great and powerful from within. With your physical feelings, you are able to feel the physical things, but with your spirit, you able to feel the spiritual things as far as a person's emotions. You are able to feel sadness, happiness, excitement, joy, love and peace. All these things you are able to feel, but most importantly, you are able to see all of these things. For all these things that one can see, it is I.

DEEP WITHIN YOUR SPIRIT

Know the spirit that is within you. The spirit of the illusion has a need to pretend and plays with your emotions and your feelings. This illusion has come very quietly and disguised itself in the things that you love. It pretends to be beautiful. It pretends to sound beautiful to you, but the whole time you are dealing with an evil spirit. You listen to music and say it sounds amazing. What you do not realize is that the sound coming from the music is a low vibrational feeling that is pulling your spirit down. Then we begin to listen to the words and feel they are helping our spirit but not knowing that the words are destroying us. While we are listening to this music, we are in tune and even know the words to the song, but it is destroying your spirit as you sing the song word for word. We say we are high vibrational spirits, but we are truly low vibration spirits. Understand so one day you may know that what you are listening to and the things that you have seen on TV or social media are destroying your spirit. It is a false feeling that the system is trying to sell to get something from you.

You think you need these things in the physical but not realizing that there is something on the other side that is taking a feeling away from you in exchange for an evil feeling. This spirit will begin to package this thing up to make it appear beautiful. It could be an attractive woman or an attractive man. The illusion will package it up so beautifully that you believe this thing was made for you, but it is an illusion. The feeling that you are trying to accept is exchanging the feeling that you have, which is a good feeling, for an evil feeling. An evil feeling will begin to embrace itself into your spirit. So, you ask, how does this evil spirit exchange its feelings with your loving spirit? Take for example the things that you have wanted for a long time. You may have said to yourself over and over, "If only I could have a beautiful wife," or "If only I could have a handsome husband." These things will come to you in a beautiful package. It will dress nicely. It will smell nice and even look nice, but the exchange is not an even exchange. What you are prepared to receive is an evil energy, a feeling that you do not want. You have exchanged your energy with this other being for something beautiful to get something evil and of a low vibrational energy.

Later in life, you begin to see that what you have exchanged was not a fare exchange. Eventually, you become depressed, not knowing that the energy that you are feeling was the energy that was exchanged from the other spirit. That other spirit is feeding on your energy to try to uplift its own spirit and keep its own life intact with its own lifestyle so it can do what it chooses to do in this illusion. You have taken on the exchange of the evil feelings of the other low vibrational being. This is the spirit of taking on the feelings of an evil entity. You must really pay attention to the feelings that we have chosen to exchange. What you have chosen to exchange is not an even exchange. You have chosen to exchange with an evil entity that has packaged themselves up so well and so beautifully that you think what you are receiving is something good but not realizing what you are receiving is really a low vibrational energy that is trying to destroy "you." KNOW THE SPIRITUAL FEELING THAT IS AROUND YOU.

BALANCE OF SPIRITUAL ENERGY

To balance spiritual energy is when you enter a place and the energy in that place is at a low vibrational level. Anything can happen in that place. When you have people in a place that are not working on fulfillment of their own spirit, they are moving toward the void. Anything and everything can happen in that place. But on another side of this, if you bring someone else into that place who is working on a high vibration of I and working on their spirit and uplifting people, this person is moving toward growth and growing from within. Not the physical but the spirit of itself. This person is moving towards positive vibration, and if this person enters a room, this can actually cause balance within that place. This can keep everybody at a place of calm, a place of somewhat peace, not a true fulfillment of peace, but a small amount of peace for a short period of time while that person is in the room. Once you start losing certain spirits that are at a place of growth, this will cause negativity to enter that place. It enters that place because that person's energy is at a low vibration, and that low vibrational pull can also pull you down to a place of low vibrational energies. This low vibrational pull can also cause a reaction, even to the point where a person could lose their life if they are not careful. This is why it is very important to raise your vibration. This goes back to the subject about feelings and collecting certain feelings and good energies that you have noticed and have studied from within. Collect those positive energies and those spirits and keep those energies with you. The feelings that you choose not to accept, speak to yourself to release those feelings. You choose not to have such a feeling from within, but you choose to have a feeling that is of your own free will. This is power. This is real power. To understand and to know thy self, to know your true self; not the physical but the spirit. The more we know our spirit, the better off we are with the journey from within.

Everything in the illusion has a spirit in it. If you have the spirit to listen, you are able to feel that other presence. No matter what you see in this illusion, it will talk to you—the birds, the bees, the trees, the plants, the animals. Even the things that you least expect such as the mountains, the wind, and the ocean. If you have the spirit to listen, then you are at a high vibration that is moving towards greatness instead of towards the void. You are able to see and feel and hear that other spirit that is present around you. You are able to feel the spirit. Do you feel the presence of that other spirit? Can you feel that presence? Can you feel the presence of the animals you own? Are you able to feel their spirit? They are able to feel your spirit. This is the reason why they are so happy to see you. That dog or cat is able to feel your spirit. So, I ask you again, are you able to feel the presence of your environment? Are you able to feel the presence of the people around you? Are you able to feel the presence that is in this place? Are you able to feel the presence in the air? Are you able to feel the presence of the ocean? Feel the presence. Take the time to feel these things. Feel greatness. Feel that great and powerful energy, those things that are all around you. A man is only strong when he is able to feel all things. A man is weak when he feels nothing. When you can feel the presence of all things, that is powerful. That is a man who should be treated like royalty, like a king, and even like a god. Know who you are! Know the presence that is around you. All things you desire, or need will be brought before you because you have a spiritual connection with all things.

We should take heed of all feelings that have been presented to us. All feelings that we have experienced, we need to take notice because it is the understanding of the feeling that you are feeling. And when we understand the reason why we are feeling the way that we are feeling, a lot of this begins to make more sense to us. Things start to become a little clearer to us. When we understand the experience of the feeling, then we understand the all, all creation, all things. This is what your life is about; it is much bigger than your physical self. It is much greater than that. It is much more powerful than the things that you love in this physical reality. It is much greater than that. Life is abundant. Life is beautiful if you make it so. Life is horrible if you

41

allow it to be. You are all that you choose to be. You are all feelings and emotions that you choose to own. This is what is leading you — your feelings. You determine and make decisions based on your feelings. Your feelings are making you do certain things. Some things you are only doing because a friend wants you to do so or maybe you want to do as you please. But with these feelings, you are only doing these things because you feel it is a part of you, a part of your spirit. This is why you choose certain things. Maybe because you have experienced it before, or maybe you have not, but it is all a part of your experience in life to know thy self, to know thy ways, to know thy will and to know thy commandment. For all that you do, all that you are and will be, it is I.

A person who looks for value in the things of this world, who looks for the material things of this illusion — like money and jewelry — to make them happy, who looks for value in other people to make them happy, has a weak spirit to look for value, but we should know that we are that value. We are that power. It is us that brings value. Value has never been in the material things on a physical level; value has always been in your spirit. You have all that you need within you. You are the diamond. You keep looking for a diamond to purchase, but until you realize that you are the diamond, you will continue looking for value outside of yourself. You are that value, not this physical value, but what is in your spirit. Your spirit is priceless; your value is much higher than this illusion. Your value is much more powerful than what this world can give you. No one can pay you for the value that you hold; you are priceless. No dollar figure can match you in this illusion. Your value is infinite. A person who looks for value on a physical form is dealing with a state of depression. Stop looking for value and become value—that is you, and that is I.

DARK SPIRITS & LIGHT SPIRITS

When the spirit leaves the body, that spirit is either going to be a dark spirit or a light spirit. A dark spirit is a spirit that has been living within a void. The spirit that I have been living in is the darkness. The darkness of not knowing thyself, not learning thyself, not understanding thyself, not acknowledging thyself. A dark spirit is a spirit that is lost. A dark spirit is a spirit that does not have control over its own life. A dark spirit is misguided. A dark spirit has blinded its eyes to where they can't see or hear what is in I. But a light spirit is a spirit that is full of light. A light spirit is a spirit that is pure, a spirit that has spent time knowing thyself. I spend time learning thyself, understanding and acknowledging who I am. A light spirit knows where it will go after it leaves the body. A light spirit is a spirit that is free. A light spirit is a spirit that has no limits, no boundaries. A light spirit can only go up. A dark spirit is going backward.

When you are spending time with yourself, the spirit is constantly getting lighter and lighter to the point where it is full of light and life. A spirit that shines upon thee when it is in your presence. You can feel their presence, and you can see the vibration when it enters the room as it shines as a bright light. Sometimes that spirit can shine so bright it can give a person in darkness a little light and allow them to see just for a moment. This is the difference between light spirits and dark spirits. When your spirit leaves the body, you will either have a light spirit or you will have a dark spirit.

This is why it is very important to know thyself, to know what kind of spirit is in you, that is in I.

CHAPTER 4
THE FALLEN ANGELS

You serve the beast and evil spirits when you worship in religion, show the signs of the hand, eat the food of the dead, to bow down, to worship, to speak the wrong language, to not have love.

The fallen spirits of the fallen angels have come in many forms. Do you see the evil spirits that control the bodies of the people? Do you see it? Well, if you do not, you should look a little closer. This evil spirit is very mysterious; it moves as a snake. Its purpose is to destroy whoever chooses to worship it. You must openly invite this evil spirit in. So, you ask, how do you invite this evil spirit? Well, if you are in religion, this is a form of controlling your spirit by these evil forces, which is hidden to the physical eye. The evil spirits are in every religion made to hate one another because they are not of the same religion. The evil feeds on evil energy in all its forms. Be incredibly careful of the things that you partake of or worship. To worship is to become a slave to a master or an idol of the flesh. It is time to come out the womb of the mother and come up into the spiritual world, but not of the dead. These evil spirits come in many forms such as greed, sickness, drugs, alcohol, sex addictions, religion, lying, killing, false love, false peace, false happiness, false joy, false teachers, false information, false history, false books, false language, false race, false titles, false leaders, and in a false life.

The world you are living in was made by the fallen angels. A world that comes to you through the illusion. The illusion of your vision, the illusion of your feelings, the illusion of the fantasy. You see, the world we are living in was made up by the fallen angels, by these fallen spirits that have chosen not to leave this universe, this galaxy, or some of you may say, this bubble. The fallen angels come to you with many kinds of addictions. Addictions such as drugs, alcohol, sex, greed, and so on. These demons are low vibrational spirits. Spirits that have not found their way or understand their way. These fallen angels are coming to you with the things that you love, the things that you adore and the things that you want. These fallen angels are quiet, very sneaky. They are very precise as they try to manipulate, deceive and control their victims. This demon that a lot of you are faced with is not your own. It is not you, but it can become you if you have chosen for it to be. This fallen angel that sits along the side of you is coming to destroy you.

These fallen angels are not allowed to leave this universe. They are kept here until they raise their vibration. They are bought back and reincarnated into physical bodies or a lower vessel to repeat itself.

Until then, that spirit is wandering across the earth, across your place of worship, over your household and with your sickness. This spirit comes to you as not only a challenge but also as a great test. Know thy sheep by the fruit that they bare. A lot of you are hypnotized by these fallen angels, by this illusion. This spirit has taken you away from yourself. This spirit has brought you to a place of pause, a place of sadness, a place of weakness, a place of sorrow. The spirit has taken you to a place of hunger or a place of needing a blessing, a place to need help from someone. These spirits are coming to you in many shapes and forms. Forms that you or I do not see all the time. It can come to you in a beautiful way, or it can come to you in a way that is evil, in a way that is not of your approval. These spirits are coming to you in many forms. They are wandering across the earth with the things you are suffering from—the alcohol that you crave, the drugs that you crave. These spirits are working with you through your addictions. The things that you love is what this demon is after. So, you love, so you shall be.

This demon has no heart. It only cares about itself. It only sees its own self due to the fact that it needs to leave this bubble because it is miserable. It has been held down because the vibration is low. This is why we must raise our vibration. As long as your vibration is low, this spirit has the right to enter. Not because it wants to enter, but because you have allowed the spirit to enter your body. Once a spirit enters your body, it has control over you, believe it or not. It can

47

control even your thoughts, your darkest secrets, the things that you are curious about. These demons will enter your body and explore. They will have a pity party in your body as a tabernacle. This demon does not come to give you peace; it comes to give you sorrow because the demon is miserable and is upset that it is a low vibrational entity and cannot leave this universe or this planet. It will play with your emotions, your feelings, the things that you say you need and the things that you love. This spirit comes to attack; it comes to destroy. This demon is not your friend, but it pretends to be a friend to you or even a best friend. It may even pretend to be a brother, sister, mother, or father.

This spirit has no heart. This spirit has no feelings. This spirit does not care anything about you. It only wants something from you. It only wants one thing from you because it needs to raise its vibration. The spirit is feeding on your energy as a battery that needs to be charged. It goes to weak spirits who have fallen for addictions, the spirit of lust, the spirit of sadness and depression. The spirit wanders in your body as it needs a home. It will not only wander but it will get close to friends of yours. It will go through you to get those friends so it can lure others into doing acts of evil. This spirit is roaming around in the air, but the eyes cannot see nor can the ears hear because, where there is space, there is a spirit. I say again, where there is space, there is a spirit.

The best thing a person can ever do in life is control his or her own mind. The day that you lose control over your mind is the day that you allow spirits to enter into your body. A man who does not control his mind is a death to his own soul. We were given all the things we need to survive. For as your mind, for as your arms, your legs, your feet, and your eyes. You have all the tools that you need. Even if you do not have both arms, legs and all of your fingers, you still have your mind. As soon as you lose your mind, you begin to lose yourself. The most powerful thing a man can do is control his mind, his thoughts, his vision, and his decisions. To be or not to be, to choose to be free, is choosing to be happy. These fallen angels are not free, but they would like to be. You see, in order to be happy, you have to be free. Real freedom is happiness within your own self. To be at a place that is limitless is to be free. Having no boundaries is to be free. This is the real you. The moment you let go of your freedom, you have become a slave for these fallen angels. You have become a slave for the fallen angels to deceive your thoughts. To deceive you into being a drug addict, to deceive you with being an alcoholic, to deceive you to being lustful as a married man, to deceive a woman to being lustful and mistreating her husband. These demons will deceive you into doing wrong amongst your kids, family members and friends.

These spirits have no heart as you may have. This spirit is upset at you, but it cannot harm you as long as your spirit is at a high vibration. But if you are at a low vibration, the spirit will enter your body and have its way. This is its purpose. The spirit is not your friend. It will continue to try to be your best friend, but it is not your friend; it is an illusion. You may see a friend or family member acting crazy, but it is not them. Maybe there is a low vibrational spirit inhabiting them which allows them to act in such a way. We think it is the person acting in a strange way, but in reality, it is this evil spirit. This evil spirit roams as the air roams the earth. This spirit is not your friend. It will never be your friend. As long as you are in this body, it is unhappy, it is upset at you.

On another note: this spirit can become you. It can become part of your spirit if you become comfortable with this evil spirit being upon you. If you are comfortable with reacting at someone because they yelled at you, you react back to that evil spirit not realizing that it is an evil spirit that is acting up. We tend to act as the evil spirit acts by getting back at someone as a man with a gun, so he uses it as well as the second man, so now you have two evils. He is the same as the man who used the gun the first time. The spirit that was in the first man moved to the second man to do the acts of evil. Again, we tend to get comfortable with this evil spirit that will soon become us. This evil spirit will become you if you allow it to enter your home and your family. If you allow this spirit to have its way in your life, you will later become the same spirit that you say you do not want to be. There is nothing new under the sun. So, it is so, and so it shall be. So, it is you, and so it is I that you see. The world of the fallen angels is a mystery in itself; it is a master in this illusion. We must understand the type of spirit this is.

So, you ask, where did this demon come from? How did this demon appear in this illusion? Why is the demon here, and who created this demon to be? Well, one day, there was a man who was married to a beautiful woman, a woman with whom he spent a lot of time, a woman he loved. They were focused on being in love in the illusion, while he spent his time trying to make all the money in the world. Trying to become richer and richer, greedier, and greedier. Not realizing that real life has nothing to do with money. The man continued to live his life pursuing his dreams, goals and his passions thinking that this was real life, that this was true success. But oh, my friend, it was nothing but an illusion that was given to him by the system. And the system continues and continues to repeat itself over and over with the same formula, and these beings continue to wander in the same place. To think that life is about money, cars, how many houses you own, how many businesses you own or how much money you have in stocks. These things are the fantasy. These things are the distraction to growth in your spirit.

But through the eyes of the man, he continued to live and became richer and richer, but his wife began to wander because the man soon found himself being too good for her. He began to sleep around on his wife, and the wife began to sleep around on her husband. They continued to live this fairytale of being married within a fairytale. The

51

man continued to get richer and richer and take from people, rather than give to help people. He took from people who needed it the most. As time went on, the man continued to get richer. Soon, the man decided to divorce his wife for another woman who would please him while he was in his so-called "success." The new woman pleased him, but after a while, he grew tired of her and began to wander and cheat on her, and the woman began to cheat on him because of his pride. The man had so much pride that he talked down on other people who he viewed as beneath him. That spirit became bolder and bolder. It began to have more pride as time progressed. This spirit began to wander off from its true purpose in life. That spirit began to involve itself in things that were not legal and other things the man should not have been involved with.

The man continued to do wrong toward other people, not realizing what he was doing to others was all going to come back to him one day. Some of you may think that what is coming back to you will come to you in this form or this body that you are in now, but it does not always work that way. Some things come back to you after the spirit leaves the body. This is when you realize the importance of what real life is and what true life is. It has nothing to do with the physical world. The physical world is an illusion to what the real world is. We are caught up in this illusion, not realizing that our spirits are not being fed. As a plant is been fed food, water, and sunlight, so shall the spirit be fed the minerals and the things it needs to survive in this illusion. The real you is a spirit. When we get away from this terminology, this is where we find ourselves going back into the void. This is where we find ourselves not being fulfilled. This is where we find ourselves being reincarnated back into the body or to a lower vessel, whether it be a dog, a cat, a bug or even a rat. The things that you hate, you could one day become. We tend to think only about this physical body but not realizing that life is on many levels, and the illusion is on many levels. Life is much more than how much money you have in the bank or the type of clothes you have. We realize that these things are foolishness when it comes to the spiritual world. These things have no meaning. These things were given to you by the fallen angels.

Going back to our story, the man continued to live his life. One day, this man walked across the street and got hit by a car. The man's body flew across the sky and hit the ground. His spirit saw his body against the pavement. The man's spirit began to wonder what he was seeing. He thought he was living life when he was in the body but did not realize that the purpose of life while he was in the body was to get the experience to know and grow the spirit to get out of this dimension and this bubble. Soon the man's spirit realized it was outside the body and that it was too late. As the spirit tried to reenter into the body, he began to think about all the time he had wasted. He was upset at himself and was lost living within the void. So, his spirit began to wander the earth.

(Note: There is nothing wrong with death, to go into the next life because everything and everything must go. A good spirit will choose to leave in peace, while an evil spirit is forced to leave in sadness or anger. But understand there is a great difference in torture. To be torture while leaving from one life into the next is an impure spirit that has lost its ways. A spirit that has not found itself or does not know who I am. It does not know the power of I or choose to know.)

People began to see this spirit appear to them. They became afraid of what this spirit was. They were afraid because, when it appeared to them, it was a ghost. But the spirit was the rich man who mistreated his wives, the man who mistreated other people and was only concerned about his own money. The man was unhappy so he wandered the earth and began to haunt the people because he was held down here on earth and could not go anywhere until he raised his vibration to another level. So, the man continued to wander the earth hoping to raise his vibration. If he could not raise his vibration, he had the choice to enter another body on this earth. The man eventually had to enter another body and redo the experience over again. What he did not realize was, when he entered into the new body, the things that he felt and knew while in his old body were soon forgotten and wiped from his memory. He could not remember what he was before that because he was in a new body to see a new experience.

The man was now in the body of a woman who grew up to be a nurse. The woman was a good woman, but she looked for a husband to take her away from her job that she hated. She wanted to be at home, and she wanted the man to spend time with her, to take care of her and give her the attention that she needed as a woman. So, one day, this woman found what she was looking for and became a wife to her husband. She did all that she knew to please her husband. She spent time with her husband, she cooked for him, she treated him right. She was faithful to her husband, but her husband continued to mistreat her. She could not understand why she was constantly being mistreated. She did everything she could to make him happy, but she continued to be mistreated. Before long, she thought the relationship was going somewhere, then her husband ended up divorcing her. Her husband divorced her to be with another woman. She was devastated and heartbroken. She was in pain. She could not bear the feeling of her husband leaving her to be with another woman. She did not understand. She began to cry out to her God and asked why. Why is this happening to me? What have I done to deserve this?

Years later, she met a new man, and she thought he was the one. She decided to move on from her old husband and get with this new man. All was going well until her new husband came home later than normal one day. He came home with a scent of perfume on his clothes. The woman smelled his clothes and noticed the scent was not from a man but from a woman. So, she confronted her husband, and he continued to lie and said it was nothing. She knew deep down inside that her husband was with another woman. The situation continued until she decided to file for a divorce. The woman did not realize that all these things that were happening to her was due to a prior life she once had. She was repeating the cycle.

So, you see, this system that you live in is being run by the fallen angels. As a man looks for a wife, the man focuses on the woman while the woman focuses on the illusion. The woman focuses on the physical things in life that spark her eyes. The things that get her attention like a nice car, a nice house, money, jewelry, and so on. The things that cause her to forget that she is in the world of illusion, to forget that nothing in this illusion exists. Everything is a fairytale. Nothing is real in this illusion. As for the man, he intended to get all these things to be wealthy for the woman he loves. He intends to do whatever it takes to get these things, and so does she. These are the things that cause most of you to be held back and reincarnated back into this illusion. This is being hypnotized by the system and its ways. The ways of the illusion is a twilight zone. It is an illusion that most of you are being hypnotized by, not realizing what you are seeing is all a distraction from what your goal truly is in life. The only purpose you have in this universe is to get the experience and grow your spirit so you can raise your vibration to a higher level. To not to understand this is to be held back into the void. To be held back into a lower dimension, a lower form. This is the world that you are living in.

Your emotions and feelings are being fed on by low energies that are taking all your energy. This is the purpose of this illusion made by the fallen angel, to feed on your energy, to feed on your pain; it needs this energy to survive. The only way it can survive is to feed on human energy. Can you see it? Do you feel it? Can you see this evil spirit that roams in the air? Again, where there is space, there is a spirit. It can be a lost cousin, a lost friend or whomever it chooses to be. They are nothing but different forms of energy that are all over the universe, and they are stuck here until they raise their vibration. These are the fallen angels. These spirits are unhappy and unsatisfied where they are. Raise your vibration while you still have time. The world you are living in is not something to play with. The world you are living in is an illusion, a test for a better you.

HOPPING SPIRITS

The impure spirits tend to hop inside your body. They do this during the times when you have forgotten about yourself, when you do not see yourself, when you do not understand yourself, when you do not have control over yourself, your mind, your body, or your spirit. These impure spirits will find the right time when you are most vulnerable to hop inside your body. When a person says, "I don't know what happened or what gotten into me, but I was not myself,". The spirit they were at, at the time was a low vibrational spirit. These spirits tend to play tricks on you. The spirit that was playing with you while you were drinking was a playful spirit. It had you at a place where you laughed and joked and played. You thought this spirit was you, but the whole time, it was a spirit that entered your body when you least expected it. You had a drink, you kept drinking, but you did not realize that you had too much to drink.

Maybe it was during the times when you started doing drugs and you found yourself getting high, but you wanted to get a little higher. You found yourself being away from yourself. You found yourself wanting more drugs. So, you became addicted to the drug that you were taking because you were caught up in the way it made you feel. It made you feel good, so you allowed that spirit to keep playing with you. You allowed that spirit to have a pity party inside of your tabernacle. You allowed that spirit to act its way. You allowed that spirit to cause you to be an impure spirit. Then you started to lose things. You started to lose your wife, even your kids did not want to be around you because of your addiction. Not realizing it was the spirit that caused you to act in such a way. It was an evil spirit that entered your body that you have not noticed. It jumped into you when you least expected it.

Maybe it was during the time when you had an argument with a friend or a stranger. The stranger made you so upset, that it caused you to lower your vibration to the level of the stranger to the point where you wanted to fight the stranger. Not realizing that you have lowered your vibration so much that you allowed that spirit to enter into your body. You might have even caused harm to the stranger, maybe to the point where it caused you to go to jail due to your uncontrollable spirit or your uncontrollable emotions.

This spirit has no remorse; it has no heart. This spirit will jump inside you when you least expect it. Therefore, it is important to watch the company you keep. The places you go and the music that you listen to all have a repercussion on your life and your spirit. Be careful of the decisions that you make for the road ahead.

SUBSTANCE

When you smoke certain substances that are of the flesh or the physical world, you are pulling evil spirits inside your body and blowing out the good spirits that are within you. You are blowing out the good spirits and inhaling the things of the physical world. To understand and to know this is to have spiritual vision. This is where the eye can see the illusion. A man who does not have spiritual vision is blinded to the physical world as well as the spiritual world. When you put certain substances in your body, you are inhaling low vibrational spirits. You are putting these spirits inside your body, and you are telling yourself, "This is good for me; this is ok for me to do," because you are caught up in the flesh of your worldly ways of thinking like the system. To be at peace is to be in the spirit of love, not to be in love but the spirit of love, then you will begin to see that you have been warned. The curse that is upon you, upon your body and your spirit is a demon that is trying to destroy you. This is why you must awaken and get out of this illusion while you still have time. The feeling of alcohol and drugs is an illusion, a false sense of happiness. To feel good temporary and later to only feel bad, to feel sad, and to feel depressed. It is only an illusion, a trick to get inside your spirit and fulfill its purpose of the flesh. Open your eyes so you can see the things that are surrounding your spirit, of your illusion. The things of your world and the things that you have created that is of the flesh.

MEDITATION

We must be careful when it comes to the spirit of meditation. When you meditate, you are relaxing your body and your mind and opening the door for spirits to enter into your body. This is a fair warning. Let me say this again: when you relax your body in the spirit of meditation, you are opening the door for spirits to enter into your body. So, you ask, how do you allow these spirits to enter your body? Well, you are releasing control of your mind. When you release control of your spirit, you are allowing something else to come in and operate your body, your tabernacle, your house. This place shall be sacred. Let me say this again: this place in your tabernacle shall be sacred. When you allow other entities to enter your body, you allow these other spirits to come in and have a pity party in your tabernacle. The spirit of meditation has come to you by the system. The system has given you the spirit of meditation so you can have other entities to enter your body. This is the reason why they promote meditation in the system. It is a way to lose control of yourself and allow someone else to gain control over your spirit. This is not the way to live life. In life, you should gather information and the understanding of the data to live and to move forward.

Real life has nothing to do with this fake meditation that you call peace, with the sound of music to open your spirit up for other spirits to enter. This is nothing but an illusion. It is a trick by the system to get into your soul. Be extremely careful about who you allow in your tabernacle, in your house. Be careful because the body is sacred. This is a warning to your spirit. The best meditation to lift your spirit is to speak to yourself with affirmation. To talk to the soul part of you is real power, abundance, and spiritual growth.

The spirit of trying to be a celebrity or entertainer, a singer, a rapper, whatsoever you choose to call yourself in this illusion. A lot of you are trying to be the best you can be in this illusion. You are trying to be the best singer, the best rapper, the best actor. Well, one thing is for sure, the system was made for you. The system was made for the people who are influenced by the system, the people who are under the spell by the system, the people who are hypnotized by the system. In order to be a great actor, you must become the character. So, you ask, how can you become a great actor or that great character? Well, let me explain. To become a great actor or that great character that you are portraying, you must bring forth that spirit of this earth, which is the fallen angel, to enter into your body to portray the character that you are trying to be. Whether that character is a bad guy or a good guy, you must allow that spirit to enter into your body to become that character that you have chosen to be. This is the same as meditation. The actor closes their eyes and says their lines over and over again. This is the same as presenting a spell to a person. To present a spell, you are repeating words over and over. An actor repeats their lines over and over to become the character and bring that spirit into existence.

As a rapper or entertainer, a lot of you are influenced by the system. The system has allowed you to manipulate the majority of the population with this music that is a disgraceful form of creation. This music that is leading the young people and this new generation to a lower vibration. So, you ask, how is this rap music influencing the population and the majority? First, when you listen to this type of music, the intent is to get you with a nice sound, a nice tune, a sound that you like that sounds good to your ears, but when you listen to the words they are saying, the words are violent. It is designed to destroy your spirit, to lower your vibration, to kill your brother, to promote violence, to promote drugs, to promote alcohol. The people who are promoting it get the big checks, and the people who listen to this music are acting this music out as an actor. An actor listens to that evil spirit so as the listener who is listening to this rap music that sounds graceful to their ears. They listen to this music and portray the lyrics and pretend to be the character that they are listening to. They intend to act like the character including using a gun, drugs, and alcohol. Some of these rappers you know of today do not even use these things they are promoting. They are only promoting it because the label they are signed to tells them to promote this nonsense.

This illusion to the majority is to lower the vibration because of the energies that are being portrayed and being sucked up by low vibrational beings that are over the society that we are currently living in. The music is destroying the community like a bad disease, like a sickness that is spreading in the community. All these things are part of the illusion. This is why you must get out of this nonsense of this music, these movies that are destroying the people and the characters that everybody worships. You see these so-called "good movies" with superheroes, but even the superhero goes around destroying and killing people. Anything good does not need to destroy anything. Evil destroys evil. It takes evil to destroy evil. Good does not need to destroy anything because good is to be at peace. In order to be evil, you have to become the same spirit. Once you understand this philosophy that evil is a low vibrational force that's content in its ways, it does not change, and it refuses to grow on a higher vibrational level. Evil is designed to go against the grain, but it is also designed to help you see the good in this life. You would not know the good unless you saw the bad. Nor would you know evil unless you saw the good. Light reflects darkness, and darkness reflects light. You must have both in this low vibrational universe. A shadow is seen in the light to fulfill its true purpose.

Understand that the beast is trying to conquer you. The beast is trying to destroy you and is watching your every move. The beast sees you, but do you see it. The beast is looking for you. How can you conquer this beast? How can you destroy the beast? To destroy this beast, you must realize that you could very well be the beast. This beast is not your friend, but it is pretending to be. This beast is at a low vibration. The beast has no heart. It only cares about itself and only sees itself. We must understand the type of demonic entity that it is after. We must understand what we are dealing with is nothing to play with. These demonic forces are roaming in the air. These demonic forces have no heart. They are out to destroy you. These spirits are out and are running out of time.

Where we are today, life is not what it used to be. People are not who they used to be. Love is not what it used to be. There have been a lot of changes happening in this universe. A shift has taken place within the universe. There has been a change within the people of the universe. The vibration has gone lower. The vibration continues to get lower and lower in this dimension. The people use to have a heart, but now man has become the beast. They have become this demon which they have tried to get away from for many years. They have now become this demon, not realizing that the demon is them. You ran from this beast for so long and refused to face this beast that you have become the beast. You have walked in the footsteps of this beast. In your ways, in your heart, in your actions, you have become this demon that you have ran from for so long. This evil spirit is nothing to play with; it is a demon that you are entertaining. You are entertaining this low vibrational entity. To play with this evil spirit and its evil ways is to play with fire, and eventually, you will get burned. You have become the fire that you have ran from for so long. Now you must release yourself from this evil fire and its evil ways.

The lower your vibration becomes, the less you can hear the words and feel the energy of greatness that is within you. You are not able to feel that magnificent power because your vibrational level is so low that it does not understand and refuses to feel this power due to its disobedience and the ways of the system. This disobedience will cause you to destroy yourself without anyone else involved. This spirit of pride will cause you to destroy your own spirit due to your own disobedience. Then, later in other lives, we ask ourselves why this is happening. What have I done wrong for this to happen to me? The spirit of disobedience is not freedom. The spirit of disobedience is to be held down as a slave. The spirit of disobedience is to be held down by the physical world, the system. This is not your home. This is not your tabernacle. This is not your true self. This is not your spirit. This is a low vibrational force that is pulling you to a lower dimension. True life is freedom; it allows you to be free. Not to be held down by an evil spirit and true happiness is to be. True happiness is within you; it is within I, within thy self, within myself, within I.

CHAPTER 5
SPIRITUAL HEALING

I would like for you to do this step with me so we can get rid of these spirits that are in this place. These spirits are hiding amongst you. I would like for you to say this commandment with me and to yourself with great power:

If there is any spirit in me that is not of a freewill, that is not of peace, that is not of real love, that is not of real happiness, that is not of a pure spirit, I command for thee to go this day. I command for thee to leave my tabernacle this day. I command for thee to go back where you came from. This is my body. This is my mind, and I am the king of my own throne. I hold the power of my own tabernacle.

If there is any spirit that is wandering inside of me trying to create the spirit of sickness, I command for thee to go. I command for thee to free yourself from this body. You are not welcome here anymore. You are not welcome in this tabernacle, and you are not welcome in this place. I command for thee to flee. If ye choose not to do so, I command that all of thee to be put upon thee this day.

If there are any spells placed upon me, I command that these spells be released this day. I command that these spells go back where they came from, and the spirits they are trying to put upon me, I command for thee to flee, to free yourself. I have control over my own mind. I have control over my own spirit. It is my freewill, and it is my right. For I AM GREATNESS. I AM POWER. FOR I AM ALL POWERFUL. IT IS I THAT YOU SEE, AND IT IS I THAT YOU DON'T SEE. I command for any spirit that is not of freewill, that is not of love, not of peace, not of happiness, that is not pure to free yourself this day. Release my tabernacle. Release my body. Release my mind. You have no power in this house. Release yourself this day. I command that these things shall be done WITH ALL THE POWER THAT IS IN ME, FOR IT IS I.

Spiritual healing is to let go of everything you feel in the physical world, in the world of the flesh, of this body and of things that we define as love. We must lose this way of thinking, the ways of the system, a system that is unclean to your spirit and your soul. This thing that is floating in the air is as unclean as a virus, which one must let go. One must let go of this physical feeling that you are faced with, this physical body and this physical mind. We must lose this false sense of the illusion because what you are seeing is not real. The physical has dressed these spirits up to get your attention and lower your spirit in how you feel and view life. Life is made by the illusion to be this way, and if you do not have this, you have not reached your full potential in this false hope. What do we do when we do not get the physical things we want in life? We start to feel sad. We begin to look down on other people, not realizing it is a void that is in I that needs to be fulfilled, a void that is miserable and unhappy with life and for other people. With this spirit comes other spirits who come to play with your emotions along the way, spirits that encourage you to feel bad, to feel sad, to feel hate for others, and hate for self. These kinds of spirits will lead your spirit to a place that is unhappy and not fulfilled. The kind of spirit that is always in need of a blessing. A mind to feel as if he or she is not all powerful, that all that I am is in me. That all my physical desires are nothing but my flesh. That your physical way of thinking is made by the system. One of the biggest ways to lose yourself is with this physical mind, with these physical visions that put you in a box. A box to feel that you are always in need. To feel that someone must save you, someone must help you. Real power is to realize that no one can help you but you. This is your free will as a free spirit that must possess himself from within. All that you need is within you rather than the outer world. It is on that inner world of you to feel the way you choose. You must correct this false sense that you are seeing from day to day. You are in control of this destiny and your next destiny. This includes feelings, pain, needing to feel accepted by this world, to feel accepted by your mother or your father, yourself, or your mate. Sometimes it is better to be free than to hold on to the things that you love.

RAISING YOUR VIBRATION

One of the most important parts in spiritual healing is raising your vibration. If you truly want to heal yourself, you must raise your vibration. This is important when it comes to having a pure spirit and a pure heart. In the world of the illusion, we are taught the system, we are taught to be a robot. But understand, to raise your vibration is to completely change your lifestyle. To change the way you think and how you currently live. Ask yourself if you have the type of spirit to help others, to give to others. Free yourself from the mindset of the system, that has program you to only care for self. This is a curse of the system, to care about self only and not for others. The mind to give to others and to help others to be free from the system. Connect with the universe and become oneness with giving because the spirit of giving can destroy evil spirits that you may have within you. Evil does not like to give; it takes from others. To truly connect with all things is in the spirit of giving. What are you doing to connect to the universe? To connect with the birds, with the insects, with the trees, with the plants. Life is about giving. Life is about growth of your spirit. What you do outer, you do inner. This is the most important things in life, it is to grow your spirit.

If you really want to be a positive man or a positive woman you should first start by helping others. A man that helps people, also helps himself because when you are in the spirit of giving you are releasing demons out of your spirit. You are releasing the spirit of greed, the spirit of anger, and the spirit of pride. Another form of raising the vibration is uplifting other people. Uplifting other people or your brother or your sister. To always speak kind words amongst your brother, always speak the best for others as you would choose for yourself. If you want the best for yourself, then put out the same to others. A great man is a man who always has something good to say, even in a bad situation. A great man will remain positive amongst negativity in the world. A man who is great and positive, so is his spirit great and positive. A man that is great and positive, so is the way he eats and takes care of his body. The body is the tabernacle. If a man does not take care of his tabernacle, then he does not take care of his spirit.

To take care of your tabernacle is to watch the foods you put in your body. Watch the foods that are of the dead. The foods you put in your body are to be the green herbs, natural plants from the earth. Food should be placed in the body to rejuvenate the body immune system and give the body the energy that it needs. Anything other than this is destroying your spiritual energy and growth. Drink only the purified water of the earth because anything else is of the flesh. Be careful of the things that you eat and the things that you drink.

Another form of raising your vibration is watching the things you view. Watch the things that the eye can see. Be careful what you put your eyes on because this can lead you to a world of destruction. What you view your eyes on, you also put your mind on. What a man views he also put his mind and spirit on. This is something that we must pay close attention to. Watch the things that we look at if you want to raise your vibration.

Another form of raising your vibration is to pay attention to the music that you are listening to. The sound that you are putting in your ears should be words of positivity to uplift your spirit. Uplift your spirit with positive words. Get away from all the negative words in the music and even in the sound. Watch the spirit of sound because certain sounds have certain energies, and certain energies have certain sounds to put you in the spirit of low vibration and depression. Be very careful of this type of spirit of sound.

Another form of raising your vibration is surrounding yourself with positive people who are connecting with the universe and are working on spiritual growth. If you want a high vibration, you must be careful of the company you keep. The company pertains to the levels of energy. Certain people in your life can lower your vibration by their negative energy or the negative conversation, the negative mindset or thoughts, the negative ways of the system. Stay far away from people who will lower your vibration.

Another form of raising your vibration is to get into nature, to go to the ocean and speak affirmation into your life. Speak words of power into your life, make things come into existence in a place that you find to be of peace. This is particularly important because what a man speaks, so is he.

The final way to raise your vibration is in silence. The spirit of silence is immensely powerful because this is where you can talk to yourself, to find yourself and to listen to your inner self, to feel the real power that is in you, that is in I. Talk to your inner spirit for answers and concerns that you may have, but remember, this is the final step after raising your vibration from the system's way of thinking. Know thy self, the power that is in you, that is in I. Shine upon thee with your light. Shine upon thee with your love. Shine upon thee with your peace. You must become the light so others can see. You are protected by your light. Understand so one day you may know.

ENERGY SHARING

Another way vibration is raised or lowered is energy sharing. Sometimes a lot of you are sharing your energy without knowing it. A person with a low vibration tends to look for energy with a higher vibration unknowingly because that person may be sad, unhappy, or depressed. That spirit will look for another spirit to feed on, to raise its energy, its level of consciousness because the only way you can survive in this life is to raise your vibration. As I stated earlier, the only protection that you have is your light. Where there is no light, there is no protection, there is no happiness, there is no peace; there is only confusion. To raise the vibration is to be around things that will uplift your spirit. Sometimes you will find that people with a lower vibration will come around you more often to collect your energy to replenish their own. It is as if you are sharing your power with someone else. They use you so they can uplift their own spirit so they can be happier because they are at a place that is unhappy and sad. They need that extra energy because they feel weak. They feel lost because to be at a low vibration is to be lost; it is to be confused because they do not have any light to share. Therefore, it is especially important to keep a high vibration and work on thy self instead of worrying about others. The more you work on self, the more you will build your own vibration and do not have the need to feed on others for a temporary fix. To have the power to raise your own vibration is real power, that is everlasting.

LOVE THY SELF

The world that we are living in has given us this false sense of what love truly is. It told us that love is to be with a person, and we have the power and the right to hold onto that person. That we have control over that person and their every move. Every decision they make, we find ourselves being in love with that person. We find ourselves telling that person to do a certain thing, to act a certain way, and if they do not do so, we are disappointed, heartbroken, sad, and miserable. This spirit of love has people thinking they have the right to what a person has, but this is an illusion. Real love is to allow a person to be free. To be in the spirit of love is true love, and that is freedom. When you do not allow a person freedom, then you are putting them in a form of slavery, but you are also putting yourself in a form of slavery and bondage. This spirit of love has come to hold you and put you in bondage as the religion. We must heal ourselves from this false belief and allow people to be free. Allow a man and a woman to be free. What good is life if a man is not free?

The same goes for religion. We must heal ourselves of the false beliefs of these religions that were given to us by the system. It was based on history or his story. It was based on traditions back in the past, even in past lives. These stories were talked about in the past along with the past prophets that were all given to you by the illusion. We must heal ourselves of this illusion and let go of the religion. All that you need, you must go within yourself and bring it out of you. If you have a problem with anything, you must face the problem within yourself. If you do not face the problem, you choose to leave the problem, you choose not to have the spirit of growth. This is a part of spiritual healing. You must face the problem because where there is a problem that is not faced, the situation stays the same. If nothing changes the person, then he will remain the same and remain content. So, in order to change and grow on a spiritual level, we must face the problem. When you face the problem, you are growing your spirit. This is one of the reasons why you are here on this planet, on this earth, in this dimension, in this bubble, in this system. This is one of the reasons why you are here—to raise your vibration. We must raise our vibration. Again, I say, if you have any problems or any issues, you must face the problem as the human being that you are. This is a part of your free will, to think for thy self, to understand for yourself and to get it with time, whether that time is a year from now, five years from now or ten years from now. It is your right to get it and understand it for yourself. This is what your free will is.

As the creator of all things, you have the free will to choose whatsoever you want to be, whether that is to be a slave or to be free. But, if you truly want to experience spiritual healing, you must release all the pain that you feel for others. Allow others to think for themselves as I. You must release this pain that you feel for other people. Release that pain today. Let it go while you still have time on this earth. Release that pain that you are feeling or that pain will carry to your next lives. This is why it is very important to let go of any emotions and feelings that you feel towards anyone. Everybody is growing on a spiritual level. When you have reached that spiritual level, you are then taken away from this body as your spirit and moved to a higher vibration that you cannot imagine. When you have not reached your full potential, then you are left here and reincarnated back into this body or a different body until it is corrected. This is the purpose of life. Life is made for you to grow your spirit. Let go of all things that you feel about other people. Let go of judgmental spirits because, as a high vibrational being, you will understand that you were once there in a past time or even a past life. You were once there at that void. It is time for you to come out of your mother's womb. To grow up and get into your spirit, where you are able to walk, run, and eventually, fly as your spirit. Let go of all these things that you feel for your family, your brother, your sister, maybe your mother or your father. You must let go of these spirits. This is all a part of the void. Let go of that spirit this day. It is your right; it is your free will to be free in this dimension in this physical experience. Let go of all the pain that you feel. Let it all go. Let go of the pain that you feel from a lost family member because you will see them again when they have reached a higher vibration as I. You will soon see them again. All is spiritual energy. If we understand that all that we see and all that we are is nothing but spirits and energies, life itself will make a lot more sense to us.

We must let go and create positivity, raise the vibration, give to others, help others. When you give to others, you are feeding your spirit. As a plant is growing with sunlight and water, so shall your spirit be fed. In order to feed your spirit, you have to give to others. Give to your brother. Do not take from people but help people to grow on a spiritual level. Life is not about pride. Life is not about who is doing better than who or how much money you have. Life is made to grow your spirit on a higher vibrational level so you can leave this dimension and get out of this void. Real life has nothing to do with this physical illusion. Let go of all this social media, this false illusion, this fairytale in this illusion of being or how many followers or friends you may have compared to someone else. This spirit of competition is an evil spirit that is like a disease destroying people before their eyes. This causes the spirit of depression and brings forth the spirit of hate, which is deadly to your soul. Wake up and get out of your mother's womb. It is time for you to grow up into the powerful being that you are. You are great. You are greatness. You are powerful. You are in the form of all things. You are the power in everything that you see and everything that you feel. You are all things put into one just separated into the physical form. Get out of your mother and come up into a beautiful, mature being that you are.

You have all that you need within you. Any blessing you want or need, you already have. No one can bless you but you. You alone have the power to bless yourself. No one can save you. You have the power to save yourself. This is your free will. This is your right. You are all that you are. You are the creation of all. It is you that you feel. It is the pain that you feel from past lives. You have come back to this life only to feel that great pain again today. Let go of all the pain that you feel. Let it go this day. You have the power to free your mind, to free your spirit, to free your heart of all the pain that you feel. Let it all go this day. You are in the power of all. You are in the power of all things. Be free, my dearly beloved. Be free, for I am free, so will you be free. You are all that you are, and I am all that I am. I have made you to be, and you have made me to be. You are an extension of I, and I am an extension of you. Let go of all that you feel because what you feel, it is I.

It is I that will release all the pain that you feel in your life. It is I that will humble you and ease your spirit. It is I that will make you abundant. For it is I that stands before you. For it is I that has allowed you to be free. For it is I that is all around you. For it is I that has allowed you to be. For it is I that clears all your thoughts. For it is I that will make you whole again. For it is I that is you. You are a king. You are a free spirit that enters the body. You were given this life, and you will leave this body to go into the true life or the spiritual world and will enter back into another body that you will call life or another form that is presented. All for your experience, all for your will, all for your desires, all for your life, and all for your glory. You have chosen all the feelings that you feel, so you have the power to let go of all the feelings and pain that you feel. Be free while you still have time. Be free while you are here in this life. Live life happily ever after because a man who is happy in this life is happy ever after in his spirit.

It takes great spiritual discipline to make yourself happy, to make yourself feel good. It takes great discipline to make myself happy. I must allow myself to make someone else happy, and that is to give. When you give to others, you respect all life in all its forms. This is when you realize what true happiness is. To respect all life is to understand life, the life that is presented before you. You are in control. You have the power to make things what they are. You have the power to change the way things are. It is your great purpose that you have chosen. It is your desire. It is your freewill, whether that freewill is holding you or allows you to be free. Life is about experiencing new lives, new chapters, new beginnings. To begin something new is to end what is old, and to end what is old is to do away with what is old and enter into something that is new. To enter into something new is to go inward. To leave something old is to go outwards. To exit what is old and enter what is new is life.

If you are not growing spiritually, you are going backwards and not outward into what is new. To understand this is great power and great understanding. To know this is to know who 'I' am. To truly know who you are and where you came from, not some biracial name that was given to you by the illusion but to have true, everlasting life. To have true, everlasting life is to have love, and to have love is to be free.

We should respect and appreciate all life that is in this world because it is a part of you; it is a part of I. What you kill you will soon become, and what you become you will soon live. The things I love I once was, and the things I hate I have never known. Parts of I are parts of you, and for all parts of you, it is I.

CHAPTER 6
CREATION

For we are one of the same spirit, broken up in infinite pieces and given freewill to create...

One of the greatest tests in life is money and time. But what if I told you, I am my greatest test? What do I choose to be? What have I created? Who am I? What have I become? I must examine myself and recreate myself to a higher me, which is a spirit of peace and love that is being fulfilled. For within the time, we create the moment. For within the time, we create the test. For within the time, we create the illusion. Understand so you may one day stand to know the truth. To know the what, which is the creation. What is the purpose of this creation? What is the fulfillment in it and to whom? For as a seed is planted and multiplied, so is the creation that one must possess from within.

Live for creation not in creation. For it is I...

So, you ask yourself, what is within me? Where is this great power? First, we must feel the moment. We must feel the past, and we must feel the spirit. I am here as part of the creation. I am the seed that was planted and replanted. For I am of the same spirit given freewill to create whatsoever I choose. Ever since I was in the womb of my mother, I have created. Ever since I was a child, I have created. Ever since I became a man, I have created, and today, I create. For creation is a part of me, it is something that is in my spirit. It is something we all have, but sometimes we must lose ourselves from the world, from this curse of evil spirits who have chosen to be. It is the curse of the illusion that got you away from yourself; it is the curse that you have chosen not to see. Awaken to your true self, which is creation. Awaken to your true self that is peace, that is happiness, and that is love, which is fulfillment. Get away from the void, which is the curse. Love yourself; love who you are and what you are. Create a new world, a place of your own peace. The world that you are in, you have created in a past life. The things you like, take it with you to your new world or create something new. The power is in your hands. You have been made to create. Feel yourself, feel your own power, and feel your spirit. Go on, feel yourself. Breathe in and breathe out. You are life and have the power to give life. Life is in you and all around you; it is yours. We are living in a world of creation, look around you. It is beautiful if you can see its power. I have lived in many worlds, and I have created many lives in past lives. Some good and some bad but lives that I have created for myself. Life will only give you what you give it. If you do not want it, then you should not create it.

What do you see or what have you chosen to see? What you are seeing is only a small part of your next creation. This is the start of your next creation. It does not matter what I say, it's what I see. It is ok to speak, but if we never see it in the spirit, then all we have are words. Words only mean something if I see it in the spirit. Some of you have been creating things unknowingly because of your vision. We ask ourselves, "Why did this happen?" Therefore, it is important to know thy self. Knowing yourself gives you the power to take control of your own life and the outcome.

This life has taught man to fear and to want but not to have. Evil is upon you. Evil is upon this world, until we recreate the world we are living in. It is moving towards a lower dimension that is moving towards the void. We must lose ourselves in the way we do things. It is a curse. THIS BOOK COMES TO YOU AS A GREAT WARNING. As a seed is planted and life is created, as a man creates his son or his daughter, this is your seed. We must be careful with the things we create and the things we leave behind, for we reap the things that we have planted and see the things that we have forgotten.

THE FORGOTTEN SEEDS

There are some things that I have said that I did not mean to say. There are some people that I have hurt unknowingly, that I did not mean to hurt. These are forgotten seeds that were planted without cause, but those seeds were planted. In life, we are made to create no matter what. If we are in a good mood or a bad mood, we are creating things we want and things that we do not want. Maybe it is something we might have seen on the media or from a friend. Maybe it is the people who we choose to be around or family. Any of these things affect your spirit and cause you to create in all circumstances. Your power is all around you, the good and the bad. Listen to yourself. Feel yourself and the great power that you possess. Life talks to us, and we talk back by our actions and the things we create in life. This is given to you as freewill to choose whatsoever you desire. Heaven is only something that one creates for self, knowingly and unknowingly. Not a place of the world or its religion unless one accepts the power of another spirit and that other spirit becomes a master of that weaker spirit. You have the power to control your own outcome; it is up to you to do so.

The power of feeling is connected to the vision, which is creation. The feeling and the vision work together as the arms and legs work together. Feeling is so important when it comes to the vision. Everything you want in life is based on feeling, not the things that one may see but the things that one may feel. The power of feeling is more than you could ever imagine. It can make you feel good, or it can make you feel bad. The feeling is where I begin to create the things I want and the things I do not want. Life is all about creating to see the vision and to create the feeling.

There are five powerful feelings that every living thing has and will experience. One of the most powerful feelings is love. It is a feeling that brings your spirit to a remarkably high place. Love brings your spirit to another place, a place everyone has experienced in his or her past lives. Love is timeless and strong and is one of the most beautiful feelings anyone can have. It is also the feeling that connects to happiness. Love is a feeling that we want to last forever because it is forever. The second most powerful feeling is hate. Hate is a feeling that takes your spirit to a place that is exceptionally low. The spirit of hate is also connected to the spirit of sadness, which leads to the spirit of anger and then leads to violence. Hate is a feeling of your lower self. To see the good, we must see the bad. Hate is a feeling you should always avoid. The third most powerful feeling is passion. Passion is a powerful feeling that comes from the soul part of you. Something new that is created by the All, by the one creator of everything. Passion is a feeling that puts your spirit at a high place. Passion is another feeling that feels timeless because it is timeless. Passion is a feeling that puts you at a place of peace and in tune with the creator. The fourth most powerful feeling is sex. Sex is a feeling that takes you away from the physical body and to a place in the spiritual world with another spiritual being. This feeling is so powerful, if not the most powerful because it has the power to create life. Two powerful beings that come together have the power to create life itself. The fifth most powerful feeling is fear. Fear is something that everyone is afraid of but do not know why. Fear is a low state of being. Fear is your lower self. Fear is something that stops you from overcoming self. Fear is an immensely powerful feeling that has the world at a place of fear. Fear is a feeling that keeps you from growing into knowing thy self.

When the power of vision and feeling come together as one, it goes into another form of the creation. All things that were made, good or bad, were made with spiritual vision and spiritual feeling. Everything you do not want is being made out of your fear and your vision. This is where your power lives, on the inside of you. As a seed is planted and multiplied, so is the creation that one possesses from within. The seed from the creator is you being multiplied with the things you have created in your mind. Your power is at work now, whether you know it or not. It is either working for you or against you because you have not taken the time to know thy self. Whether it is your government or your religion, whatever it may be, take control over your life and regain your power. It is your gift from the creator.

In the universe we are in, we are collecting data for our own universe within. A new universe that we are creating inside of us. How do you see your universe? Is your universe of love, of peace, of happiness? Create that beautiful world and demand for this beautiful world. Take control of your life. Live in your peace and harmony. No limits and no boundaries. I choose a world of freedom with no limits or boundaries. I choose a world with no money because I know the hate it can causes but a world of giving and sharing. A world with no pain, no sorrow, a world of true life that is seen and unseen. The world that you see you must create from within. Ask yourself, what is in your world? What have you planted in your world? What seeds have you sat upon thee that you are reaping?

SEEDS= SEEDS= A SEED OF MY SEED

The secret to creating something new is darkness. When you close your eyes and think of the things you want, it is darkness. Darkness is not always bad; it allows you to create something new, something from within and something from nothing. In the womb of the mother, life is being made in darkness. In the darkness, something is being revealed, something the eye cannot see. Real power is in the darkness, not the physical world of darkness but of the spirit. The darkness is not evil; it is the beginning and the ending of something new. Free your mind from the system that programmed you to think a certain way. You are free, my dearly beloved, as I. Whatsoever you need in life, do not ask for it, create it as it is yours because you are the creator as I. Your power from within is one with everything that is and what is not. You have more than you will ever know. You are powerful as you are and connected to the all—seen and unseen. You are all within the all and is all power, all powerful.

NOTE: Understand that there are two types of darkness. There is a darkness that is good, which is creation from within your spirit. But also know there is another form of darkness that is evil due to a person who refuses to grow on a spiritual level, which is to live in the physical form of the darkness. This is the darkness that most of you consider to be evil; that is a person who choose not to grow. The darkness of creation is to make something out of nothing; this is creation. You must understand the different forms of darkness. Darkness is not necessary always evil, but it depends on the darkness you are referring to. Most people only know darkness to be evil, but again, darkness is not evil unless the person made darkness to be.

We must get out of the mind that this is always considered to be evil. If we realize that some of us are in the form of darkness as creation and others are in the form of darkness to be content or to settle, this is to live in the void. When you are refusing to grow, then you are in the spirit of hate, violence, in the spirit of making others sad. Then you are in the spirit as the void, and this is not in the form of darkness as creation. This is something totally different. Please understand this and what this is. Know yourself because, when you know thy self, you know where you are in the spirit, and when you know thy self, you are at a state of growth rather than a place of being evil.

When a person is at a state of evil but not in creation, that person is going backwards rather than moving forward. When you go backwards, you are moving away from spiritual growth. When you stop moving toward growth, then you are going backwards, you are going back into the beginning. You are going back into that place that was, the past before the understanding. You are going back to that place of nothingness, to the nonexistence. Regardless of if a person is moving away from growth, they are just going back to being nothing. The beginning of anything is creation, and once it is created, it is taught a certain way. Whatsoever it chooses to be or expects to become is also a form of the creation. If you understand this, you will understand what evil really is. Again, evil is to go backwards. So, on a deeper level, evil is not bad or evil; it is just another form of making something new. It is penetrating against what is already made, so it is just a reflection of what is already there.

What is going backwards something must move forward. In order to see what is moving forward, we must see what is moving backwards as light and darkness. When we understand this, then we will understand what life is all about. To not have life is to have life in another form. But we must see both. This is true power. This is spiritual understanding. Also understand that evil is to destroy thy self. Evil can be destroyed by itself or another form of evil. Evil is to destroy itself because in order to destroy something, you have to become it. You have to become it because if you're not evil, you won't be around evil nor will evil want to stay around you. It may come in the form of a test, but you will not condone it or embrace it because you're not evil.

Evil is only evil to the people who are evil. When you embrace yourself on a higher vibrational level, you begin to get away from evil.

You stay away from evil because you know what evil really is, and you know the type of spirit that it is. You choose to be on a higher vibrational level, a higher form of understanding of all things on a spiritual level. Become a master of yourself, and you will not have to look for a master to put you in a box to be evil.

Stop lowering your vibration to receive a blessing. Create the blessing as I have already given you power as I. You are the same as I but only in the flesh or the physical world, which is only a place of growth and understanding. This is the experience that you chose long ago before your mother had you. You have created it to be. You have entered your mother and was raised by the system that was made to take you back to a lower vibration, but it is your freewill that you have chosen. You have the power to choose your next life, your next experience or you may stay in the spiritual world as I. Do you remember this place? Do you remember your past desires? Do you remember your past lives? Do you remember the dreams that you had and how they made you feel? Do you remember the different lives that you had lived in your past? It is all of you. Do you remember the types of spirits you used to be?

Life is a journey for the next beautiful place that you create for yourself. It is your freewill, whatsoever you choose and so it is. I am creating my life with my desires, with the people I choose to be around, with the things I set my eyes on, with my thoughts, with my feelings, with my emotions, with the things that I love in the physical world, and with the things I hate in the physical world. All that I am, I once was a thought or an experience in another world.

Everything you are and was, you have created. The biggest illusion is that we were created, but the creator is you. You have created thy self, thy will, thy ways, thy likeness, thy pain, thy happiness, thy sadness, and thy power. For the creator is you, who is creating new worlds, new experiences, and new lives. A seed of a seed is I. A creator is all that I am. A creator is I.

CHAPTER 7

I

The earth is the same as I. Whatever I do in the body, I do in the earth. I am one with the universe, for I am one with life. It is up to me whatsoever I choose to create, for it is I. I have the power to do so, for it is I. I am the creator that lives within the creator. It is I that you see, and it is I that you do not see. For I am the life within all lives. It is my great power that surrounds you.

For I am a free spirit given freewill to be whomsoever I choose. I am the spirit of peace. I am the spirit of love. I am a spirit of happiness. I have a free mind, I have a free spirit, and I have a free soul. For anyone that tries to enslave my spirit, I command for you to flee. I command for you to go. I have all that I am that is within me. The creator that is within me and the creator of all things that is a part of me; it is a part of my soul; it is a part of my mind, and it is a part of my spirit. I have all that I need within me. I am happy. I am loved. I am peace. I am powerful, and I am abundant. I have all that I need within me. I am spiritually successful. I am whosoever I choose to be.

This is my will. This is my commandment. This is what I have chosen. This is where I am. Soon I will be in a place that is better than this system that we are in and this evil spirit that is trying to take over this place and this body.

I am a free spirit. I have all that I need within me. I am all that I am that is within me. This is my will. This is what I have chosen. I choose abundance. I choose spiritual power. I choose freedom. I choose love. This is my commandment this day. For all things that I am, so I will be all that I AM to whomsoever I choose. I choose when it is time for me to leave this universe. I choose a higher vibration, a higher dimension that is much greater than this. I choose a higher vibration that is much greater than this flesh with the spirit of peace and love as I. For I choose a higher vibration than this world, for this is my will, this is my power, and this is my commandment.

For I have lived in a world where I have seen so much pain. For I have lived in a world where I have seen happiness. For I have lived in a world where I have seen my joy. For I have lived in a world where I have seen struggle. For I have lived in a world where I have seen slavery. For I have lived in a world where I have seen the illusion. I have seen people lose themselves. For I have seen a man destroy himself. For I have seen love. For I have seen power. For I seen greatness. For I have seen abundance. For I have seen success. For I have seen a life that had so much pain. For I have seen friends that came and are now gone. For I have seen families who have separated.

93

For I have seen brothers who have separated. For I have seen sisters who have separated. For I have seen the separation of families due to the lack of love. For I have seen the separation of families due to money. For I have seen separation because of a certain skin complexion. For I have seen separation due to a person's religion. For I have seen separation due to politics. For I have seen separation due to education. For I have seen separation due to being poor and being rich. For I have seen all of these things that have come and gone before me. For I have seen spirits that wander the earth and have entered the bodies of people due to their comfort and content, due to their spirit of lust, due to their spirit of addiction, due to their spirit of greed. For I have seen these spirits wander the earth. For I have seen people who began to lose themselves. For I have seen so much in my life. For I have seen a world that is not like I.

For I have seen so much. For I have seen so much pain. For I have seen so many emotions. For I have seen so many feelings within a person. For I have seen a mother's touch. For I have seen a father's touch. For I have seen different gods in a world that is corrupted. For I have seen so much in the world that we are living in today. For I have seen sickness. For I have seen anger. For I have seen lost loved ones. For I have seen myself. For I have seen my power. For I have seen my abundance. For I have seen my glory. For I have seen so much pain. For I have seen a man. For I have seen a boy. For I have seen an infant. For I have seen a baby enter into this world. For I have seen an elderly man leave this world. For I have seen the changes in people. For I have seen the changes in me. For I have seen what people will do for love. For I have seen the things that people will do for money. For I have seen a world that was good but was destroyed by its greed. For I have seen so much in my years in this life. For I have seen so much hate. For I have seen a world that does not love you and does not allow you to be free. For I have seen a person lie to you over and over again. For I have seen all these things. For I have seen a world of tears. For I have seen a world of happiness. For I have seen a world of peace.

This is myself that I have seen. I have seen all that I am. I have seen all that I have created on this earth. I have seen all of myself. I have seen all of you, and you have seen all of me, and you will continue to see all of me. For all that you see and all that will be, for it is I that you see. For it is I that you feel. For it is I that you breathe. For it is I that you hear. For I am that I am. For it is I. I am all around you. I am everything that the eye can see, and I am everything that the eye cannot see. For I am all around you. This is all of me. For this is all of you. This is all greatness, all great power that is all around you. I am all that you see, and you are all that I am. For all that is and for all that will be, for it is I. I come in the good, and I come in the bad so you may know that it is I that you see. It is I that you feel. I am you, and you are me, for we are one within the same place. For we are one separated. For we are one in all things. For we are one. I am all that I am, and all that I am it is I.

FEEL THE PRESENCE

Can you feel my presence? Breathe in and breathe out. Feel your spirit. Feel your presence. Feel your power. Feel everything around you. Feel your environment. Can you feel your power? Can you see yourself as this powerful being that you are? Visualize yourself as this magnificent power. Visualize yourself on a high vibrational level like none other. Visualize yourself as being happy. Visualize yourself as being at peace. Can you feel it? Feel your spirit filling this place with peace and love. Feel yourself. Feel that everything you touch, you give it power, you give it peace, and you give it love. Feel this magnificent power. Can you feel this magnificent power that is in you? Feel yourself. Feel the power that is in you. You are powerful. You are abundance. You are great. You are glory. You are all that is in you. You are all that is in me, and I am all there is, for it is I. I am all, and you are the same as I, connected with every living thing moving on the face of this earth and many earths in many lives, in many dimensions, in many times and timeless lives. You are all things, the same as I. For I am a part of you, and you are a part of me, filled with the power that is within you. Whatever you need, whatever you want in life, just close your eyes, and create it for yourself. You have the power as I. I am everything that you are for we are one of the same life, broken up into many pieces. For we are one.

Now, look at me and tell me what do you see?

See I. See On. See I. See On. Out of this dimension, out of this galaxy and out of this place. For it is I that I see. For it is I that I feel. For it is I that is all around me. For it is I.

I AM THAT I AM…

For the world that you see, it is the eyes of I. The world that you create, it is the eyes of I. The world that you don't see, it is the eyes of I.

EYES OF

I

STEVE ELLÉ

THE BEGINNING

OF THE END

OF THE BEGINNING

MAY YOU GO WITH PEACE AND LOVE.

Made in the USA
Monee, IL
15 March 2022